PRAISE FOR *EMBRACE YOUR EMPATHY*

"If you are an empath (like me), you need this book...You've only to crack this cover and spend time with Kristy in the magical pages that follow to help yourself transform the 'terrible' into the 'terrific.' In fact, this book is more like a supernatural spa experience than anything else, chock full of the concepts, stories, understandings, and tips that will help you embrace your empathic gifts and turn them—and you—into a shining light."

—Cyndi Dale, bestselling author of
The Spiritual Power of Empathy

EMBRACE YOUR
Empathy

ABOUT THE AUTHOR

© Ellie Frances Photography

Kristy Robinett is one overachieving, oversensitive, overdramatized, over-sarcastic empath of a Scorpio. She's a psychic medium and author who began seeing spirits at the age of three. When she was eight, the spirit of her deceased grandfather helped her escape from a would-be kidnapper, and it was then that Robinett realized the Other Side wasn't so far away.

As an adult, she was often called upon by the local police department to examine cold cases in a new light and from a different angle. She gained a solid reputation for being extremely accurate at psychic profiling and giving new perspectives on unsolved crimes. It was then that she began working with a variety of law enforcement agencies, attorneys, and private investigators around the United States, aiding in missing persons, arson, and cold cases. In 2014 Robinett appeared on a one-hour special on the Investigation Network (ID) called *Restless Souls*, spotlighting a police case she assisted on. She has also appeared on a Japanese television series and on the Gaia Network, and she is an often-called-upon media commentator.

Robinett teaches psychic development and paranormal investigation lectures across the country and has a popular YouTube channel. She is the author of several books, including *Born Under a Good Sign*, *Journey to the Afterlife*, *Tails from the Afterlife*, *It's a Wonderful Afterlife*, and more. She is a wife and a mom to four adult kids and several animals. She and her husband have a podcast called *The Robinett's Nest*, voted one of the best in the Detroit area. She enjoys gardening, cooking, and front porches. You can visit her online at www.KristyRobinett.com.

EMBRACE
YOUR
Empathy

MAKE
SENSITIVITY
YOUR
STRENGTH

Kristy Robinett

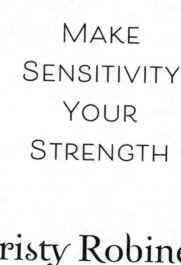

LLEWELLYN PUBLICATIONS
WOODBURY, MINNESOTA

FIRST EDITION
First Printing, 2022

Book design by Samantha Peterson
Cover design by Shannon McKuhen

Llewellyn Publications is a registered trademark of Llewellyn Worldwide Ltd.

Library of Congress Cataloging-in-Publication Data
Names: Robinett, Kristy, author.
Title: Embrace your empathy : making sensitivity your strength / Kristy Robinett.
Description: First edition. | Woodbury, Minnesota : Llewellyn Publications, 2022. | Includes bibliographical references. | Summary: "Down to earth and easy to use, this book reveals the many gifts of being empathic and how using your empathy can heal yourself and those around you"— Provided by publisher.
Identifiers: LCCN 2021049027 (print) | LCCN 2021049028 (ebook) | ISBN 9780738759555 | ISBN 9780738759616 (ebook)
Subjects: LCSH: Psychics. | Sensitivity (Personality trait);
Classification: LCC BF1040 .R625 2022 (print) | LCC BF1040 (ebook) | DDC 133.8—dc23/eng/20211104
LC record available at https://lccn.loc.gov/2021049027
LC ebook record available at https://lccn.loc.gov/2021049028

Llewellyn Worldwide Ltd. does not participate in, endorse, or have any authority or responsibility concerning private business transactions between our authors and the public.
All mail addressed to the author is forwarded but the publisher cannot, unless specifically instructed by the author, give out an address or phone number.
Any internet references contained in this work are current at publication time, but the publisher cannot guarantee that a specific location will continue to be maintained. Please refer to the publisher's website for links to authors' websites and other sources.

Llewellyn Publications
A Division of Llewellyn Worldwide Ltd.
2143 Wooddale Drive
Woodbury, MN 55125-2989
www.llewellyn.com

Printed in the United States of America

OTHER BOOKS BY KRISTY ROBINETT

Born Under a Good Sign

It's a Wonderful Afterlife

Journey to the Afterlife

Messages From a Wonderful Afterlife

Tails from the Afterlife

To all the feelers feeling alone in this crowded world. I believe in you.

Contents

DISCLAIMER

Although the stories in this book were real-life occurrences, some names and identifying details have been changed to protect the privacy of the individuals involved.

In the following pages you will find recommendations for certain essential oils. If you are allergic to any of these oils, please refrain from use. Do your own research before using an essential oil. Each body reacts differently to essential oils, so results may vary person to person. Essential oils are potent; use care when handling them. Always dilute essential oils before placing them on your skin, and make sure to do a patch test on your skin before use. Never ingest essential oils.

This book is not intended as a substitute for the medical advice of physicians, psychiatrists, or therapists. Readers should consult a physician and/or therapist in matters relating to their health and/or mental health, particularly with respect to any symptoms that may require diagnosis or medical attention.

Acknowledgments

I pitched this book project years ago, and it was wholeheartedly supported by everyone at Llewellyn Worldwide. Then real life happened, and I began to doubt my intuition and my gifts. It was like I was purposely untying my own shoelaces to trip over them. Thank you to Bill Krause, Terry Lohman, Anna Levine, Kat Neff, Nicole Borneman, and especially to Amy Glaser. Amy, after so many books and so many years, so many tears, tantrums, and late-night whining, I can't tell you enough how much I appreciate your friendship, encouragement, and intuitive wisdom.

Gratitude to Chuck Robinett, my husband and co-host of our podcast *The Robinett's Nest*. We've been through so much, but like Karen Carpenter sings, I pray that "We've Only Just Begun." Thank you for your devotion, support, and continuous smiles.

I am the luckiest to be a mom to my "kids" and bonus "kids." To Micaela and Caleb, Connor and Serenity, Cora, Brian, and Benjamin (Tiger), and Molly and Kyle, you are my most favorite "job" and I'm proud of each one of you.

Thank you to Gayle Buchan, who has supported and loved me like a best friend and a mother figure. Words cannot describe how much your constant encouragement has helped me find my path.

Thank you to my assistant Jamie Radcliffe and to Liv Baker for keeping my business operational, and for staying ever patient with me and my late night emails.

To half of the Core4, Marjanna and Mikey, I'm so grateful for late-night chats, early-morning coffee with more milk than coffee, fun Disney trips, getaways with way too much luggage, and silly conversations about the strange and unusual. I'm so grateful for our friendship.

To SUP (Special Unit Paranormal), made up of Mikey, Marjanna, Chuck, Jan, Kathy, Lynn, and Ryan. It takes a special friendship to sit in dark and musty buildings with haunted dolls and swearing ghosts. We fight like family but love bigger. I'm so glad I get to have those crazy experiences with you.

To all my clients, friends, readers, listeners, and fans who've stood by my side through life's crazy journey. Without you and all your love and support, this book would not have been written.

Introduction

If you've ever been told you are too sensitive, you are probably an empath. If you cry during Hallmark movies or if crowded places make you feel anxious, you are probably an empath. If negativity overwhelms you or you can easily spot someone fibbing, you are probably an empath. Many people think empaths are weak (including most empaths themselves), but empaths are the strong ones. Empaths carry around everyone else's feelings.

I'm an empath. If you feel it, I feel it. When I leave myself vulnerable, I feel what the world feels. When an empath is tired, sick, depressed, or grieving, the empath often unknowingly opens themselves to feeling every emotion. Those emotions stick to the soul. It's icky. It's scary. It's dizzying. It causes panic and fear—exactly the kind of energy that negativity needs to flourish. Negative energy doesn't want us to know that we have our own "weapon" called positivity and healing.

An empath feels everything deeply. A hard look can sometimes be as painful as a physical punch. Witnessing something embarrassing or violent can raise strong emotions, even if the situation was seen on television or read about in a book. Empaths are often compassionate, understanding, and overly considerate people. But when they don't understand their gift, an empath can grow bitter and resentful.

FEELING ALL THE FEELINGS

Once upon a time, there was a girl with long blond hair and blue-green eyes. You could look at her a certain way and she'd either swell with joy or crumble into sadness. She lived in a house filled with heavy emotions. The world around her was weighted and worn, and she carried it all as if it were her job to do so. She was both untaught and unable to take the time to feel her own feelings because she was so busy cleaning up the emotional messes others carelessly left behind. Before she could even find herself, she lost herself.

Growing up, everyone tried to change her by telling her to toughen up and to stop being so sensitive. She always felt different. She felt alone. She daydreamed of a place where she was accepted and understood. It wouldn't be until several decades later that she realized she wasn't flawed at all—she was an empath. There were techniques she could learn to not absorb so much while still staying true to who she was. She discovered that she wasn't defective, she was gifted.

That girl was me, and if you are reading this, it's likely you as well.

· · · ·

It was the summer before first grade when my mom and dad got into one of their fights. Well, Mom fought, while Dad offered his best weapon: the silent treatment. It was a typical August in the Midwest, and my dad was watching his beloved Detroit Tigers play ball. Win or lose, Dad watched all the same, as if it were his job. He could tell you who played first base for the Tigers in 1976 in 2020, but he couldn't tell you who my best friend was in 1976 in 1976. What caught my dad's interest was what caught his interest, and he didn't care for much outside of that. It was a frequent argument between my parents, and it is likely what caused that summer day's argument too. My mom probably wanted to go somewhere and do something on one of the last good days before autumn, and my dad wanted to sit and watch the tube. And that's what he did. He simply sat motionless and emotionless in his chair while my mom did what she did best: ranted and raved in between sobs.

"I'm just going to kill myself then," she called out to him. "Then you'll be sorry," she added, as if this might change something in the current moment.

Instead of diffusing the heightened situation, my dad looked through my mom, continuing to watch the baseball game. With one more hardened glance at my dad, she looked at me.

"You either kill yourself with me, or you stay with that heartless man," she said, her arms flailing as she offered her ultimatum.

I just stood there, frozen by her offered choices. When I didn't say anything, she shook her head in disgust, running out of the door and slamming it behind her with a hardened exclamation mark that shook me.

"Please, Daddy," I begged. "Please go after her."

Just as my mom was invisible to my dad most of the time, so was I. He continued to sit, staring, not even acknowledging that I was talking to him. Even at that age, I was a natural mediator, and I did what I thought was best in that moment: I ran after my mom.

After what felt like miles (it was only a mile), I caught up to her. She was looking over a bridge at the jagged rocks and rushing river water underneath. I could physically feel her heart breaking, and I'm not even sure she knew why. I felt every bit of her various emotions in every part of my body. I wasn't worried about me. She wasn't really either, if I'm being transparent. I did, however, worry about her.

The energy of intensity shifted to one of peace and something told me nothing would happen to us. Thankfully, the angels and guides intercepted before anything tragic happened. My mom somehow tripped backward, away from the bridge rail. It was as if it jolted her aware, at least for that moment in time.

After that episode, my mom was admitted to a psychiatric ward, but nothing helped her live again. Not shock therapy, or medicine, or therapists. Not her husband or her kids. She survived until she was sixty-eight years old, but between her mental illness, autoimmune illnesses, blindness, and finally, her heart issues, she never truly lived. It wasn't that she didn't want to; she just wasn't given an understanding or any tools to help her.

My mom's story isn't an uncommon one. Not only am I an empath, but my mother was too. The heavy emotional burdens she carried were treated as a scarlet letter, except instead of publicly wearing her mark on her sleeve, she wore it on her heart, like many empaths do. Being an empath can be humiliating and a burden, just like that scarlet letter. Being an empath was misunderstood then. It's often misunderstood now.

My mom was thrown into a psychiatric hospital every time she had a meltdown, and that taught me to hide. It taught me that all negative feelings would be punished, so I tried to push my own feelings back into the emotional closet. The more I pushed, the more I felt. It was a constant tug-of-war, like putting on jeans that

4

are two sizes too small: they might fit over your tummy, but you won't be able to zip them. It might feel practical to fit into what the world thinks you should do and feel, but at the end of the day, it creates more of an imbalance. It's exhausting and uncomfortable.

For years I had others telling me to stop being so sensitive, including my own mother! That is like telling someone with blue eyes to stop having blue eyes, or telling someone who hates liver and onions to just like it, or telling someone who is depressed to stop being depressed. Being an empath is part of the emotional wiring of the soul and the spirit, and it takes conscious and continuous maintenance.

Think about roses. When a person wants roses in their garden, they carefully choose the type of rose and where to plant them. For the roses to blossom and be healthy, though, they have to be tended to. In return, the plant's gift is years of roses. Planting roses is much more rewarding than waiting for someone else to gift you roses. Just as a rose can be picky, needing the right amount of sunlight and the right kind of dirt, an empath is complicated and needs to be tended to in order to bloom.

Sure, not everyone understands roses, and they might try and call you out for liking them. "Daisies are better than roses!" they might say, because daisies can grow in any kind of dirt, even in the middle of a street if they want to. And while daisies are pretty cool for what they offer, so are roses. There's no competition.

But an empath who isn't confident in who they are spends a massive amount of energy and time making everyone else happy. Others' opinions dilute their own wishes or dreams. "Daisies are better than roses, so why even spend the time, energy, and love to make my roses beautiful?" the empath will lament. The roses that were so wanted will then begin to wither and die, aching all the while to be loved and to provide their beautiful petals and sweet fragrance.

You, dear empath, are symbolically that rose, and just as any gardener will tell you, it's imperative to tend to your garden to get the best blossoms. Your feelings matter. All feelings matter. My goal in authoring this book is to help you find the tools to be the beautiful rose you were born to be. And if you are a daisy or an iris, that isn't weird or unusual; it's cool to be different.

ONE
All About the Empath

When you tell someone that you are an empath, it's often met with curiosity and a "You mean you have empathy?" But being an empath is different than having empathy.

Empathy is the capacity to feel or understand another's feelings. Someone might share they lost a loved one, and someone with empathy shows their compassion with words or even a hug as a sign that they understand the emotion the other person is experiencing. Although an empath has empathy, anyone can be empathic.

An empath is someone who was born with the ability to feel the mental, emotional, and sometimes even physical state of others. The empath is a psychic sponge. If someone has a headache, some empaths can feel that headache too. Some may feel the physical pain of the headache as their own, while others may feel the emotional pain that the headache is causing or the emotional pain that may have caused the headache. If someone shares a loss, an empath will feel that loss as if they themselves are experiencing it through some or all the senses of the person with the loss.

Empaths feel the need to be caregivers even when they don't want to, even when their own soul isn't being tended to. Yet they have an amazing ability to heal from tough situations, and empaths sure know what tough situations are. They will run into the emotional fire, even though they know there are repercussions for that—even when they know the person they are running into the fire for doesn't want to be saved. It's because of that sacrificial type of soul that empaths feel misunderstood. They see, they know, and they sense how things are for everyone else, but they overlook their own needs.

Many empaths don't understand why they feel what they feel or even what they are feeling. The empath can become consumed by good and bad energy, all the while trying to make everyone around them feel better. They will offer others soul food while starving themselves. Collateral damage happens when a person's energy gets bogged down; this can affect the empath emotionally and sometimes even physically. Think about Pig-Pen from *Peanuts*; an empath may not notice the residual dust they've absorbed from those around them, but others do, and this can send out vibrational signals that don't speak to who the empath truly is. Empaths can get stuck in that vibrational space and align themselves with people, places, and situations that aren't conducive to their purpose. Empaths often find themselves lost in a world they never wanted, craving a world that feels different.

Empaths are simple, but complicated. Open, but closed off. Loving, but feeling unloved. They don't like to deal with things that waste their time, but they often need the wasted time to feel balanced. Small talk is uncomfortable, but not everybody wants deep and thought-provoking conversations like an empath does, and because of that, they can feel isolated—alone in a crowded world.

EMBRACE THE EMPATH IN YOU

Being true to the gift you were born with fosters the trueness of who you are. It is like a car that is being maintained but running on old tires. When the car isn't maintained properly, it may still get you to your destination, but you worry it might not. The squeak and noise may be irritating in lieu of luxurious. So, are you riding out in a jalopy or a Land Rover?

There is no "cure" for being an empath. There's no magic potion to make it go away. Those who embrace their empath gift tend to lead a more positive life, without heightened fear and doubt. People who are naturally highly intuitive operate in a different way; they tend to lead with positivity, trust, and faith instead of fear and doubt. Although some of the intuitive messages may not make sense, those who embrace this gift understand that the Universe doesn't operate in the yesterday or the tomorrow, but in the now. Worry and anxiety are yesterday and tomorrow, and you can't properly experience the now if you are unable to step forward from the past or peering too far into the future.

It is important to note that there is no wrong or right way to embrace your gift or your fresh start. By learning to trust yourself, you can speak to your true soul and grow more than you could ever imagine.

TRAITS OF AN EMPATH

There are several different types of empaths, each one with their own gifts. I will talk more about the specific types of empath at the end of this chapter. For now, let's look at some of the many signs of an empath. You may be shaking your head yes as you read through most of these signs, but keep in mind that you could be an empath even if you do not have all of these traits.

- **Aches and Pains:** Empaths often experience GI issues, back issues, and/or autoimmune disorders such as fibromyalgia.

- **Action-Oriented:** Actions speak louder to you than words do.

- **Addictive Personality:** Empaths can become addicted to unhealthy habits to relieve the stress of feeling everything.

- **Always Cleaning Up:** You cannot tolerate clutter or inorganization unless it's your own clutter.

- **Animal Lover:** Animals of all kinds are drawn to you.

- **Avoids Bad News:** If a negative news story comes on, you turn it off. Empaths can't tolerate anything that shares negativity, violence, or cruelty.

- **Avoids Small Talk:** Small talk is painful because there's no substance.

- **Caring and Giving:** You like to help others feel better, no matter what sacrifice it might cost you.

- **Compassionate, Considerate, and Understanding:** You commiserate with other people's pain and suffering, and you feel strongly about other people's needs.

- **Craves Freedom:** You love feeling free, whether by traveling, walking in the woods, taking a day off, or cuddling up in bed without any plans.

- **Creative:** You are quite imaginative, sometimes artistic. Even if it's not the paint-a-picture type of creativity, an empath can creatively think.

- **Curious:** An empath is very drawn to spirituality, the metaphysical, and sometimes the occult.

- **Distracted:** An empath is often distracted and gets bored easily. They are sometimes accused of having ADD or ADHD.

- **Fan of the Underdog:** You root for the underdog, whether in real life or in television shows or movies.

- **Feels Everything:** You don't even have to be in the same room as a person—you don't even have to *know* the person—and yet you feel their emotions.

- **Feels Others' Pain:** You physically and emotionally feel the pain of other people or animals, and maybe even trees and plants.

- **Healer:** Many empaths know how it feels to be broken, and they try to prevent everyone else from feeling that way by being a fixer.

- **Highly Intuitive:** You can sense what others are feeling and thinking. You often can anticipate their reactions to various situation and have an uncanny sense of reading people and situations.

- **Human Lie Detector:** Many empaths have an uncanny ability to tell if someone is lying.

- **Interested in History:** Many empaths are drawn to a time period different than the one they are currently in. Some empaths study history or become involved in ancestral lineage.

- **Introverted:** An empath often finds public places overwhelming.

- **Inquisitive:** You genuinely care about everyone and everything. An empath is driven to ask questions and to truly understand people and things on the deepest of levels.

- **Loved:** Although most empaths only have a small group of friends, you are likely very trustworthy and loved by many.

- **Mixed Feelings about Antiquing:** While you may love vintage stuff, empaths often have mixed feelings toward antique, vintage, or secondhand items because of the energy of the previous owner.

- **Natural Sense of Direction:** Many empaths have a natural instinct for what time it is, the day of the week/month, the weather, or direction.

- **Needs Solitude:** Because energy is felt so deeply, an empath often finds themselves in need of more me time.

- **Observant:** An empath observes everything, said and unsaid.

- **Old Soul:** You feel like or are called an old soul. There's a wisdom beyond your years.

- **Senses Weather Changes:** You can sense when a storm is coming or when the moon is changing phases.

- **Sensitive to Loud Noises:** Whether it is loud music, loud chewing, or loud conversation, empaths often have a difficult time hearing themselves think during it. Some feel rage when faced with loud noises.

- **Strangers Are Drawn to You:** Complete strangers find your light and unload their problems, stories, and emotions onto you.

- **Textile Sensitivity:** An empath often has problems wearing restrictive clothing or jewelry.

THINGS AN EMPATH LOVES

When an empath is in their natural state, they thrive. These are things most empaths love.

- **Animals:** An empath often loves animals, and animals love them.

- **Books:** Books are an escape to many, but especially to an empath. Sometimes books are an excuse to cry or smile.

- **Children:** Many empaths love babies and kids. They just get one another, and it's not unusual for an empath to be waving and smiling at babies in a check-out line.

- **Comfortable Clothing:** Textiles are important to an empath. If their clothing is uncomfortable, it can ruin their whole day.

- **Food:** An empath loves the energy of good food.

- **Holistic Healing:** An empath is often drawn to holistic, natural healing and all things metaphysical, including tarot cards, oracle cards, and crystals.

- **Honesty:** An empath loves when those around them are honest, even if it hurts.

- **Nature:** An empath loves nature. Now, this doesn't mean every empath loves to camp. Instead, it means that an empath loves how they feel when they are grounded by nature. This might be by dipping their feet in the lake, hugging a tree, or digging their hands in the dirt.

- **Sleep:** An empath loves a comfortable bed and a good night's rest.

- **Space:** An empath attracts people and animals of all spectrums of energy and can feel claustrophobic at times. Space looks different for each empath. It might be a walk in the woods or turning the phone off for a few days. Space helps an empath realign and cleanses excess energy from them so that they feel more like themselves.

- **Water:** An empath often thrives by the water, sometimes in or on the water, and is healthiest when drinking lots of water.

NEGATIVES OF BEING AN EMPATH

There is a darker side to being an empath, especially if the empath doesn't know how to properly balance energy. Since an empath can feel both bad and good, an empath can be extra sensitive to the negativities of life, which often feel overwhelming.

- **Absorbs Energy:** An empath spends so much time absorbing everyone else's emotions that it manipulates them into thinking all of those emotions are theirs, when most of those emotions aren't theirs to carry at all. It can feel draining.

- **Appears Self-Centered:** An empath feels and absorbs energy, and this can be crippling. Others who don't understand may see an empath as a martyr, a complainer, a victim crier, or even a negative person.

- **Attracts Narcissists:** If you are an empath, a narcissist will find you. It's not an *if*, but a *when*.

- **Attracts Users:** An empath often attracts the users of the world.

- **Cries Easily:** An empath cries. A lot. Over everything. Some see it as a sign of weakness.

- **Doesn't Maintain Proper Boundaries:** It's hard for an empath to say no, and they will often lay out the welcome mat for the good, the bad, and the ugly.

- **Feels Anxiety:** Empaths can be overstimulated by people and their environment. This can cause anxiety.

- **Feels Depression:** The gifts that an empath has can often be seen as weird or strange. It's easy for an empath to feel alone (or believe that it's easier to be alone), which can make it easier for depression to seep in. An empath just feels misunderstood.

- **Feels Guilt:** An empath feels guilty when they are angry, sad, or mad, and they often apologize for how they feel.

- **Feels Jealousy:** An empath loves so deeply that they can become jealous, suspicious because of all the times they've been hurt.

- **Feels Physical Pain:** Many empaths have unexplained physical pain.

- **Feels Like They Are Cursed:** An empath often loses pieces of themselves, feeling like they are stepping on shards of glass with every step, which stops them from moving forward. This can make the empath feel like they are cursed.

- **Feels Like They Are Unimportant:** An empath might believe their feelings aren't important. When our gifts are not appreciated, it can leave a feeling of insignificance.

- **Glitter-Bombs Everything:** They give their love away like throwing glitter in the air, sharing that love with everyone—the good, the bad, and the indifferent. But some people dislike glitter, and they aren't thrilled when they are glitter-bombed by an empath.

- **Has a Caged Heart:** When empaths have been hurt one too many times—when they give their love to too many of the wrong people and their heart gets broken—they have the tendency to cage their heart to prevent future pain.

- **Highly Sensitive:** An empath might believe that being sensitive isn't a superpower, but kryptonite. They can sometimes be perceived as moody, aloof, shy, stuck up, or disconnected.

- **Is Their Own Worst Enemy:** An empath tends to be their own worst enemy, beating themselves up for choices made and missed opportunities.

- **Lacks Self-Care:** An empath often forgets that being happy is okay and not selfish. Empaths are so busy making everyone else happy that they end up too exhausted to work on their own happily-ever-after.

- **Needs Space:** An empath needs a lot of alone time, and those around them may not understand.
- **Sensitive to Noise:** Loud noise—whether from construction, loud breathing, snoring, music, insistent pen clicking, fireworks, or something else—is often psychologically painful to an empath.

DANGERS OF BEING AN EMPATH

Empaths might feel emotionally compelled to respond to every emotion. They might (over)think about what they're feeling and why, or they might feel called to take action. Empaths tend to take on the pain and joy of other people in an excessive way.

Many empaths feel the emotions and feelings of others physically, while others feel emotions and feelings emotionally. When someone feels happy and positive, the empath feels happy and joyful. However, if those around them are filled with negative emotions, the empath likewise can be filled with negativity, and many will then fall into a deep depression if they don't know how to shield or cleanse themselves. These feelings can contribute to health problems in an empath.

If I am feeling stressed out or "dirty" from the day's energy, I visualize a cleansing rain of white light that washes it away. I visualize the negativity washing down a drain between my feet, and it disappears forever. If you have a hard time visualizing, you can do this exercise in the shower. Imagine that the water from the shower is cleansing you of negativity as it pours over you.

It can be debilitating to feel all the feelings. These are some of the things that make empaths scream, "Make it go away!"

- **Absorbs Every Emotion:** You absorb everything. All of the time.

- **Attracts Broken People:** You attract people everywhere you go, especially those who are emotionally fragile and lost. You tend to attract broken people and the users of the world. You sometimes become the hunted.

- **Attracts Drama:** You attract drama because you are a good listener and always want to help.

- **Beacon for Negativity:** Even if things are perfect in your world and the world around you, you are a beacon for negativity and excessive emotion.

- **Difficulty Ending Things:** You have a hard time ending toxic relationships because you tend to give everything many chances.

- **Easily Overwhelmed:** Being around a lot of people can make you feel overwhelmed; crowds, especially, can bring out deep anxiety.

- **Feels Lonely:** Because you feel everything, you may avoid being around too many people. But this might make you feel alone, and you might discover that being on your own is hard too.

- **Feels Obligated to Do Things:** You feel obligated to change the world at the sacrifice of yourself.

- **Highly Intuitive:** Intuition is a great thing, but too much of it can be overwhelming. Your intuition is always in overdrive.

- **Lots of Tears:** You cry at the drop of a hat. It might be from something sad or from something joyful.

- **Overly Giving:** Your heart is huge, and you see the good in everyone, even those who aren't good people. You want to help everyone, all the time, and it can be exhausting.

- **Sensitive:** You are called sensitive. A lot. As if it's a negative thing.

- **Shares Intimacy with the Wrong People:** Intimacy is important to you—physical, emotional, or both. You enjoy being intimate, but while physical intimacy is nice, you tend to attract narcissists or broken people.

- **So Many Emotions:** You feel an urgency to move away from the sad and negative, but you don't want to hurt anyone's feelings, so you stay and carry that back with you.

Even though there are dangers to being an empath, the positives outweigh the negatives. Maybe you aren't convinced yet, but hang with me! We have a whole book to develop tricks and tips that will help you see your empathy as a gift rather than a hindrance.

HOW TO EMBRACE YOUR EMPATHY

It can be scary to embrace your empath gift, especially if you've been surrounded by people who aren't empaths or who just don't understand (or care to understand). Being unique has never been easy, but it's also painful to hide your trueness. It's time for you to sparkle! These are some ways to help embrace your empath gift.

Be in Your Know

An empath has a rare ability to see, sense, know, and/or feel. Everybody has intuition, but an empath's intuition is multiplied and then amped up. Intuition is like a muscle that you must build and care for. It comes from an inner knowing, sometimes because of past experiences, and a psychic sense. Intuition is supposed to teach us what to do, where to go, and who to trust. Even if you don't believe you have all the information, it's always in front of you. Yet, people tend doubt themselves and create false scenarios in their head.

When an inner knowing can't be explained, we attempt to rationalize it away. The thing is, that inner knowing is a light that shines differently. It can't be explained on the level most people would like it to be. It's like when you are being asked to prove that you are in love; you can take actions that show love, but you can't prove love. You can't prove intuition either, but you can prove the power and value of intuition.

Understand How You Decipher Energy

Those who are energy sensitive react to their own intuitive instincts. Everybody reacts differently to energy. If someone who is energy sensitive has a bad feeling, they may feel it like a gut punch. Some may just have a knowing, while others may sense lower-vibrational energy by simply feeling uncomfortable. Paying attention to how you react to good, bad, and indifferent energies will help you decipher how you interpret energy.

Believe in the Unexplained

Intuition is a guidance system, much like a GPS unit. My husband often yells at the GPS, "I don't want to go that way!" He will then go his way and, more often than not, he ends up in the middle of a traffic jam. Although the way of the GPS might be a weird way, it is the right way. Our intuition will often point one way, but our stubborn will goes the other way. Trust your intuition.

Knowing that the unexplained sometimes doesn't make sense, and making nice with that, will make your life much easier. Highly intuitive people live an emotionally healthier life when they stop searching for a reason for their psychic feelings and accept that some things are beyond explanation.

FOLLOW THE BREAD CRUMBS

Following the path of intuition requires self-trust and consistency. Intuition doesn't always buzz; sometimes it hums. It often gives us the bread crumbs, and it requires blind faith to follow that path. Trust that your intuition may lead you to information you may not like—you may very well meet the big bad wolf—but this is never to harm you. It is only to guide you to a place of peacefulness.

SHINE BRIGHT

Each of us has a light within us that shines brightly. We each have a gift, a uniqueness that makes us who we are. Fear plays a role in denying our light from shining brightly. Those who trust themselves live a freer and less fear-based life. Your intuition is always buzzing in whatever way you sense, hear, see, touch, feel, or know it. Some people teach courses about intuition and empath development, but it's up to you to trust what you know. You might build this trust by asking for a sign, meditating, listening to the quiet, or taking a leap of faith.

AVOID TOXIC ENERGY

Highly intuitive people are more sensitive to energy, and that excess exposure to negative energy can literally drain an empath. If you are around toxic energy too long, you may feel fatigue and/or become ill. Toxic energy affects the body, mind, and soul. Learn how to better handle toxic energy by shielding, practicing self-care, setting boundaries, and releasing energy. This will help you be more in tune and healthier in all ways.

FIND YOUR NO

Empaths are notorious for allowing others to break the bubble of boundaries. We complain about our boundaries being crossed, but we have to set them and continue to create reinforcement. Know that if someone can't handle your no, then they likely aren't worth your yes.

FIND YOUR CIRCLE

Empaths have an unhealthy habit of attracting and hanging out with low-vibrational people, forming destructive relationships. Creating healthy, loving, and pure relationships with those who are truly loyal helps an empath be comfortable in their own skin. Setting boundaries with your understanding loved ones cultivates a truer and more intuitive you.

REACH OUT

It's common for an empath to feel overwhelmed from absorbing good, bad, and ugly energy. It's hard to decipher whose energy is whose, so an empath can take on unhealthy conditions such as depression and anxiety as if it was their own. They might also use unhealthy means to quiet the heavy energy. A therapist can help an empath identify their boundaries and help set healthy ones using coping skills and mindfulness.

Never be afraid to seek out a professional for any kind of help. You wouldn't set your own arm after a break, and the same goes for healing of the heart and the soul. Although an empath may absorb energy, they are not supposed to be a sponge or enabler. They are supposed to be supporters and guides.

There Are No Tears in the Workplace

Empaths are creative. They are deep thinkers, natural healers, great contributors, and fantastic teamworkers (even though people exhaust them). They are enthusiastic, focused, fair, compassionate, and charitable. They're also sensitive; they carry the weight of everyone on their shoulders because they feel energetically bombarded by the expectations others put on them—but mostly the high expectations they put on themselves.

I started working retail when I was fifteen years old. It was just painful. It was all too much for me, albeit I tried hard to make it work. My motto soon became, "People—not a fan." I didn't want to dip into that negative mind frame, so I figured that an office job would work best. Guess what? Offices have people in them too! Who knew? I won't bore you with my entire resume, but there was a common theme: I cried. I cried when I was mad. I cried when I was frustrated. I cried when I was happy. I cried when I was worried. I cried a *lot*. And not cute little tears, but big alligator ones where I would have to unprofessionally run into the bathroom to put myself back together. That wasn't always something I could do, though, especially when standing in front of a board of vice presidents giving a presentation on bond issues that involved giving them bad news.

"You've got to get it together," my very assertive female boss would lecture. "You've got this."

I didn't have *this*, though, but it wasn't for lack of trying.

Not every empath has the luxury of taking a job where they aren't bothered by other humans. Even though I'm now self-employed and it doesn't look like I have any bosses, I actually have lots of bosses, and those are my clients. Regardless of your field, navigating the workplace as an empath is hard. Workplace challenges for empaths involve keeping boundaries, not absorbing the stress of the energy around them, and still being themselves.

One of my friends, Joyce, works for a company near me, but she lives in another state and does her job remotely. Joyce was called to the head office by her boss, so she asked if our group of friends wanted to meet up. A dozen of us gathered at a local restaurant for dinner, but we hadn't heard from Joyce. She finally called and said she'd be there soon. A few minutes later she showed up at the table, looked at us, and started to bawl. All at once, we started the line of questioning. *What's wrong? Are you okay? Is your husband okay? Did you get into a car accident? Did a ghost scare you in a bathroom? Are your shoes too big? Did you see a celebrity when you walked in?* I mean, the line of questioning became so ridiculous that we were all laughing at ourselves. Except for Joyce. She was just staring at us, crying.

"Seriously, what's wrong?" one of us said.

"Well," she started, stopping for a moment to order a drink from the waiter, "My boss decided I needed my evaluation since I was in town. It was great. Except—" Joyce hesitated and took a long sip of the drink the waiter had dropped off for her. "Except he said I was too sensitive, and as soon as he said that I began to cry!"

As if on cue, Joyce began to cry again. And we all started to laugh, which made her laugh too, but also cry harder.

"It's ridiculous," she huffed.

The thing was, it wasn't ridiculous, and even though our group was laughing, we weren't laughing at her. We were laughing because we all understood. And let me tell you, Joyce and the rest of my friend circle are tough cookies, but we are all empaths. If we went silent on one another, we knew not to take offense because that space was needed. We also would sometimes assume we made the silent one angry, making up scenarios in our mind, but we all understood we did that too. Because we are all empaths, we related to what Joyce was going through.

Joyce felt cornered by the spontaneous evaluation and the unexpected criticism, but she was fine after our dinner, which served as a good recharge for her. Empaths can have a hard time yo-yoing between the highs and lows. It's like jumping into a mosh pit one minute and then sitting in a quiet library the next minute. It's hard for an empath to process these highs and lows, and it can be overwhelming. Empaths need time to process emotional transitions.

One thing I taught myself to do is read the room. Whether it is a boardroom, a courtroom, or a coatroom, I read the room. If it feels sad, I prepare myself. If it's mad, I prepare myself. That way, I'm not carrying excess emotion that isn't mine to carry.

BURNING BRIDGES OR BUILDING A BRIDGE?

In life, there will always be bullies. There will always be someone who tries to belittle, criticize, demean, and judge you. It rarely has anything to do with you—it is always about them. Yes, bullying is abusive, and you should not endure it, but they don't need to react either. You should never be snack food for a narcissist. Your soul is much too beautiful for the world to lose your light.

The good thing is that there are more good people in the world than bad. You have to stop offering your energy to the vampires, narcissists, and gaslighters of the world, whether it be someone you love in a romantic way or someone you are working with. By recognizing the signs of a toxic person, you can figure out what to do next. Often, you can't completely separate yourself from bullies, but by learning how to shield yourself better, you can be ready when they come calling.

My dad always taught me never to burn bridges. That advice took an interesting turn one day at work. I glanced at my calendar one morning before leaving for my office and I recognized the first name on my calendar, but the last name was a common one, so I didn't think much of it. That is, until Todd walked in and I realized that I knew him.

Years ago, when I worked in a corporate office, I was surrounded by many young wannabee executives. Some were helpers, but most were backstabbers. It honestly was adult elementary school with pushing and lying, all in the name of climbing the ladder of success. I chose not to play that game. Maybe it was because I knew I didn't want that life for my future self. But even choosing not to participate threatened some of my coworkers; Todd was one of them.

Todd and his group did everything they could to sabotage my work. The only way I can describe it is corporate bullying. I stayed strong while I looked for another job, not wanting anyone to see they were getting to me, even though they were—especially the ringleader, Todd. My last day at that job, I made sure to thank Todd for helping me know what I wanted out of life (at least at that point in time). I remember that he looked at me weird and turned around with a cocky smile. He thought he won because I was leaving.

So, when I saw the name Todd on my appointment schedule, I didn't think anything of it. Many people are named Todd. Yet here I was, breaking out in a sweat when I recognized him as the bully I had dealt with so many years back. He was sitting in my waiting room, wringing his hands and awaiting his appointment with Kristy the Life Coach and Psychic Medium.

When I decided to leave the corporate world, I opened my office using the skills I'd developed in college and through my various jobs. But opening my own office also involved trusting my intuition and the gifts I was born with that I continued to learn, grow, and develop. For years, I thought intuition and empathy didn't belong in the corporate world because it can be hard to combine them. Intuition and empathy don't always fit into corporate correctness. Over time, I realized they can go hand in hand. And when I found formulas that worked, I wanted to help others. I had no idea these formulas would eventually be helping Todd.

I took a deep breath, added a smile, and welcomed Todd to my office. He was there for life coaching advice, and he also wanted to connect with his loved ones on the other side. He didn't recognize me. I wasn't sure if I should remind him who I was, but I decided to keep things impartial. I trusted that spirit would help me with the right words and connections.

The session was beautiful and healing for us both. Todd's grandpa, his mother's father, came through in spirit. Not long after Todd was born, his father had abandoned him, and Todd's grandpa stepped in to fill the shoes of his father. Todd's mother had to work several jobs and even then, they didn't have much. It was rare for his mom to be around to attend his soccer games or school plays.

Todd said, "Growing up, I swore that I would be super successful so I could be there for my family. I wanted money. A lot of money. And because of that, I sometimes didn't do it the right way. I pushed. I bullied. I kicked people off my company island who were good people and who didn't deserve what I did to them. I want to be a better person, Kristy. I'm so worried my grandpa is upset with how I've handled life."

That was my cue to let him know that our paths had crossed. So, I told him who I was. And he cried. And I cried. And we talked about the burning of bridges and how it was a fine line. He had learned from his experiences, and I from mine.

"Please forgive me, Kristy."

"I forgive you, Todd. I've grown, and perhaps if you hadn't pushed me off your island, as you put it, I wouldn't be here right now."

"I hope we can be friends," he said.

"I think we can. Just don't hold your past against yourself, okay?"

Not all corporate bullies have stories that make their tyrant behavior okay, but there's always a story we might not be privy to. Nothing can change in our lives, though, unless we make changes. When we are angry, we often burn bridges, but that can become messy. Instead, think of anger as a controlled burn. We don't have to burn the bridge. We can walk away from the bridge and choose another path.

A Healthier Empath

Being able to tap into a person's energy and quickly download their physical and emotional ailments can be exhausting if you don't know how to put a "do not disturb" sign on your gift. It can cause stress and exhaustion that can ultimately affect your physical self. Many empaths and intuitives have chronic health problems, such as digestive issues, back problems, headaches, low energy, hormonal problems, anxiety, and depression. It's often because empaths don't know how to set healthy energetic boundaries, or they are afraid to set healthy boundaries because they don't want to rock the boat or hurt anyone's feelings.

Although being an empath is a wonderful gift, in order to keep helping others, you need to make sure you are balanced and healthy yourself. While you are busy fixing everyone else, you must also listen to your own intuition. There are many ways to keep yourself in tune.

- **Create Boundaries:** Boundaries are simply guardrails, not manipulative direction. Boundaries do not have to be controlling, but they do have to be firm so that you can set the standard for healthy behavior and communication.

- **Be Well Rested:** An empath needs solitude to shake off other people's energy and reconnect with themselves. Even through a phone or television screen, empaths can feel the energy of others. Simply by walking into a room, an empath feels the energy of others. Sometimes, an empath can feel the energy of others even in their dreams; they might feel the energy of the living or departed. During waking hours, it is important to shake off excess energy, but when it is time to rest, that should be when an empath can punch out the time clock. Getting true rest without alcohol, drugs, or other stimulants is the best medicine for an empath. Rest aligns the chakras and renews the spirit so empaths can continue to do their soul work. Going to bed at the same time each night and getting enough sleep are vital to an empath's well-being.

- **Move:** Motion can change emotion! This doesn't mean you have to sign up for fitness boxing or run a marathon. You could simply take a walk in nature or practice yoga in a studio. Whatever helps an empath escape from the noise and overstimulation of life!

- **Know What You Can Control:** You can control your own thoughts, words, actions, behavior, and feelings. You cannot control another's thoughts, words, actions, behavior, or feelings.

- **Eat Mindfully:** Many empaths stress eat, and just like movement, a healthy diet is needed for a healthy mind. Anything that overstimulates an empath can cause an already highly sensitive person to feel overwhelmed or anxious.

- **Give Purposefully:** Most empaths would give their last dollar to a stranger. They would rather go hungry than see another be hungry. An empath will always be the giver, but an empath also needs to give purposefully by considering if their actions will harm themselves.

- **Receive:** Just as they need to give purposefully, an empath is healthier when they accept assistance. The ability to ask for help isn't a typical attribute of an empath. Asking for help is hard. It doesn't feel good to an empath. They'd rather give than receive, but giving *and* receiving balances the energy.

- **Have a Calming Space:** Having a space that's clean, inspiring, and free from chaos is important for empaths. Having a space that nurtures positive energy supports an empath throughout their day. Things they love—such as plants, candles, crystals, and/or pictures of loved ones—help an empath feel connected to their space.

- **Have a Purpose:** An empath thrives when they have a purpose to look forward to. When they lose that purpose, they begin to lose themselves. A realistic calendar that shows what's on each day's schedule helps keep an empath from dipping into depressive energy.

WHY EMPATHS MIGHT BE DISLIKED

Many empaths have called their gift a curse. I prefer the word "challenging." Empaths are often accused of being "too much." This is not an empath's flaw; this is a flaw of those reacting to the empath's energy. Because of the challenges that come from being an empath, there are several reasons why an empath might be disliked.

- **They're a Mirror:** It's rare to get away with much when dealing with an empath, as they are natural lie detectors. If an empath is well protected, they know how to decipher energy, emotion, and dishonesty. They subconsciously project it back to the person, which can be uncomfortable and embarrassing.
- **They Have a High Frequency:** People who vibrate at a lower frequency level often aren't comfortable around an empath. An empath's higher frequency is too much for them, and not everyone is prepared to raise their vibration.
- **They're Sensitive:** It's no secret that empaths are sensitive. It is one of the largest attributes that makes an empath an empath. Just as some can't deal with an empath's frequency, this sensitivity can make others feel uncomfortable.

- **They Can Be Passive Aggressive:** Empaths don't like to hurt another person, even if the other person is hurting them. It doesn't mean they won't stand up for themselves, but when they do, they often stand up and run away so they are unable to feel the energy being pushed back to them (even if it might be their own energy).

- **They Go Silent:** An empath feels everything and often takes everything personally, so they go silent from time to time. This is often perceived as social anxiety, but this is one way an empath can keep themselves grounded. They may vanish to recharge themselves. My friends refer to it as going into our blankey fort until we feel safe.

HELPFUL WAYS FOR AN EMPATH TO BE BALANCED

- **Say No:** Practice that no muscle often and start setting boundaries.

- **Embrace Holistic Practices:** Utilize Reiki, massage, or Healing Touch to help make sure that your auric fields are solid.

- **Exercise Outside:** Take a hike or a walk. Immerse yourself in nature.

- **Exercise in General:** Both yoga and Pilates are great options for empaths.

- **Stomp it Out:** Yes, really. As you stomp, repeat that you are dispelling all negativity. It's another way to clear your aura.

- **Stop Telling a False Narrative:** Stop telling the same story over and over. If you are going through something tough, stop telling everybody. You are just putting more energy into the thing you are frustrated with. Instead, work on what you want to happen.

- **Cut the Cords:** Call on your angels and guides and ask them to cut the toxic cords that are keeping you tied to the past.

- **Buy Crystals:** Many crystals help keep negative energy away. At the very least, crystals can help restore your energy.

- **Brush it Off:** Brush your with hands diagonally across the body. Start with the fingertips, go down the arms, go down the legs and torso, and then throw all of that "bad" energy on the floor to get rid of it. You can visualize a drain by your feet and watch it depart.

- **Eat Healthier:** Empaths are feelers, and that includes what they ingest. The more nutrients something has, the healthier it is for an empath.

- **Use White Light Protection:** Visualize an egg-shaped sphere of brilliant white light that surrounds you from head to toe. Visualize the light getting brighter and brighter until it creates a barrier of protection around you. Depending upon your religious beliefs, you can simply say a prayer or ask for your guides and angels to continue to surround you with the white light of protection. Ask for the white light of protection to keep you free from harm and negative influences. You can also do this for others, including pets.

- **Bathe with Sea Salt:** Sea salt is used to neutralize the environment and oneself. If possible, get unrefined sea salt along with Epsom salts (you can even mix these salts with your herbs). Draw a warm bath and relax. Add your sea salt. When you've finished bathing, drain the bath but don't hop out. Instead, think of all the things that are troubling you. Visualize them being drawn from your body and draining with the water until every drop of it is gone.

- **Use Herbs:** Many herbs such as basil, lavender, peppermint, rosemary, sage, and cinnamon have protective qualities. You can set them out in a pretty dish to help absorb negativity, or you can buy incense with these herbs and burn it. You can also add these herbs to your bathwater.

- **Cleanse with Smoke:** Cleansing your space utilizing an array of herbs is a simple and powerful way to remove negative energy from an area. Place a few leaves of a protective herb in a fireproof container or an abalone shell, then light the leaves or the bundle. The flame should go out in a short time and the herb will begin to smolder. Fan the smoke with your hand or with a feather. Say a prayer of blessing of protection as you walk around. Fan the smoke around you, imagining it passing through you. As it flows through you, it draws out all the imperfections that have collected within you. I recommend going to the farthest part of your house and working toward the front, opening a window where you can draw all the negative energy out. Don't forget to cleanse closets, basements, nooks, and crannies. You can cleanse yourself with smoke daily, as it can be an extremely helpful way to keep yourself balanced and can help if you are around emotionally unbalanced people. In the past, the most common smoking herbs were white sage and palo santo. However, because of demand, there's concern of extinction. Thankfully, many other herbs are just as powerful and useful, including frankincense, sandalwood, myrrh, cinnamon, lavender, cedar, rosemary, bay leaves, and juniper.

- **Light Candles:** White candles are wonderful for removing negative energy. Adding scents to the candles such as lavender, vanilla, or cinnamon helps even more.

- **Turn up the Music:** Since we all have a vibration, it makes sense that music can help realign our soul. Play an instrument or simply put on your favorite music, then spend time thinking about all that you want, instead of thinking about what you don't want. This can help retune your space and your spirit.

- **Repeat Affirmations:** Like attracts like. What you focus on is what you receive. If you focus on the negative, you vibrationally align yourself to that. If you focus on positive, you vibrationally align yourself to that. Doing this can be hard. It can feel like a fib. But just like spending time with happy people makes you feel happy and spending time with sad people makes you sad, the more you set your alignment on track, the faster you will feel the waves of good energy in your life.

- **Create a Vision Board:** A vision board is a wonderful tool for an empath because it helps keep their life's focus in check.

- **Clean the Clutter:** A controlled environment helps an empath feel clearer in body, mind, and spirit. Once you begin to clean, you will notice your possibilities expanding.

TYPES OF EMPATHS

I am gifted with all the empath traits. It took me a long time to use the word *gifted* in lieu of *cursed* because, for most of my life, any and all of the empath traits were heavy to hold. And truth be told, I've said out loud more than once that I just didn't want to be an empath anymore. But then I discovered that I lived my best life while embracing my empathy. I thrived when mastering the light and the shadows of being an empath.

There truly is no one-size-fits-all in this world, and that includes the types and traits of an empath. While I considered the empath quality to be a curse for a long time, other empaths have always seen it as a blessing. While I like to have a small friend group with quiet interactions, another empath may like large gatherings with lots of people and noise. It doesn't mean one is better or worse than the other; it simply means we each respond to different situations… well, differently. It's not a competition, nor is there a gauge or a blue ribbon at the end that validates your empath importance. The best thing about discovering and uncovering your unique gift is that you get to find out who you are!

The following are some of the types of empaths. You may be one type, or you may have all of these qualities.

THE PHYSICAL EMPATH

This empath will intuitively sense, feel, or absorb the physical ailments of another person. Many healers and physicians are physical empaths.

THE EMOTIONAL EMPATH

This empath will intuitively sense, feel, or absorb the emotional state of another person. Many healers, social workers, and therapists are emotional empaths.

THE INTUITIVE/DREAM EMPATH

This empath is in tune with a knowing and higher awareness. They try to allow their intuition to lead the way. Many healers, police officers, and teachers are intuitive empaths.

THE EARTH EMPATH

This empath is in tune with their surroundings, nature, and the physical landscape. They feel a deep need to support the thing that is unable to defend itself. Many shamans and healers are earth empaths.

Under the category of Earth Empath are the Animal Empath, the Plant Empath, and the Weather Empath.

The Animal Empath

This empath is deeply connected with animals. Many animal empaths feel called to work for rescues, in shelters, or in any way that they can help animals heal. Many veterinarians and animal lovers are animal empaths.

The Plant Empath

This empath is in tune with plants, flowers, and trees. Most plant empaths have a green thumb and ache to be out in nature no matter the season.

The Weather Empath

Often called *geosentient*, a weather empath is connected to jet streams, weather patterns, solar flares, and moon phases.

YOUR SENSITIVE SELF IS A SUPERPOWER!

It might be hard for you to see the benefits of being an empath if you've lived your entire life trying to hide and disguise this super-power. When you have a better understanding of your value by identifying your empath trait(s), you begin to uncover your true self. This book will help you discover which trait(s) you have, and I will also share coping mechanisms, tailored meditations, essential oil suggestions, crystal suggestions, and affirmations for each empath type. When you have life strategies, you live a healthier life. Let's begin!

TWO
The Physical Empath

ARE YOU A PHYSICAL EMPATH?

1. Have you ever been called oversensitive?

2. Have you ever been labeled a hypochondriac?

3. After spending time with someone, have you ever felt exhausted?

4. Do crowds make you feel tired, sick, or uneasy?

5. Have you ever felt someone else's anxiety?

6. Have you ever felt someone else's physical pain in your own body?

7. Do you feel exhausted by angry people or feel the need to avoid them?

8. Are you chronically tired or suffering from unexplained physical symptoms?

9. When the world is heavy, do you feel it is best to just stay home?

10. Does seeing or hearing about a person or animal getting injured physically hurt you?

If you answered yes to more than two of these questions, you are likely a physical empath. You aren't crazy. You are simply someone with a gift that can be developed and better managed.

If you don't feel like you resonate with this trait, continue to read this chapter because it will help you understand someone in your circle who has this trait.

. . . .

A physical empath is someone who responds to the physical illnesses and symptoms of those around them as if they were the empath's own illness or symptoms. A physical empath mirrors the physical ailment. If someone around a physical empath has a headache, the physical empath may get that headache. An empath can manifest symptoms that aren't their own, and they often have an array of issues ranging from chronic fatigue, depression, autoimmune diseases, and mysterious aches and pains that might be unexplained or misdiagnosed for psychological issues. The more a physical empath is around large crowds or people who exhibit stress and/or anger, the more their symptoms can be exasperated.

Many physical empaths lack knowledge about protecting themselves, setting boundaries, or releasing the hitchhiking energy that they have picked up from others—or that others have piled on top of them, unbeknownst to the physical empath.

LIFE AS A PHYSICAL EMPATH

I've had a variety of experiences as a physical empath, from being urged to quit my job to taking on mysterious physical ailments to helping the police department solve cold cases.

TRYING TO FIT IN

An empath is so used to pain that they put it on just like they put pants on every day. It's not always their own pain; it might be a stranger's pain or the pain of something they saw on the news. Pain becomes so normal that the physical empath often forgets that pain shows us what needs to change in our lives. All too often, we assume pain is there to punish us, and it makes us stop in our tracks and wallow in self-pity.

Really, though, pain is telling us to move. To push through. To go do something else. *Be* somewhere else. And sometimes be *with* someone else. Pain screams that the timing isn't right, but it doesn't mean that the timing will always be wrong. This minute, hour, day, week, or month of your life is worth more effort than wallowing or shelving your dreams because they make someone else uncomfortable. Many people want to change, but they don't want to make the effort to set goals or take small steps to get there, and they often don't accept the changes that others are making either.

Years ago, I was employed by a school district. My days were filled with work that was very black and white and rarely lent itself to creativity. I reconciled state reports. I oversaw bond issues and worker's compensation. I spent a lot of my day crunching numbers and reporting those numbers.

I figuratively pushed the envelope by offering ways to make my job creative. Maybe I could write a newsletter for the staff and it would help with morale. Maybe I could help plan the retirement events. Maybe I could utilize positive training to help lower worker's comp. Or the district could start a webpage. Yeah, I didn't know how to program, but I'd figure it out, and I'd do it all, even if I had to take night classes and pay for it myself. I ached for creativity, and occasionally, I was rewarded with nibbles. I was like the little girl who wanted a puppy dog and wouldn't let up.

I think the district simply wanted to quiet my constant ideas, and after several years of trying to reinvent the wheel—or, as my boss said, constantly trying to bring the district into the twenty-first century—I was suddenly given a promotion. But the promotion stuffed me into a corner office with a computer, more reports, and no potential to add an ounce of creativity to my position.

My reward for doing so much, and trying to be everything to everyone, was becoming ill. Really ill. I told myself to suck it up. My doctor told me to look for a job that would better fit my personality and my needs, but I didn't want to be considered a failure. I didn't want to be a disappointment. I could do the job, yet every time I was feeling a tad better and decided to return to work, I got sick all over again. I could do the black and the white, but my body, mind, and soul craved colors too.

The day I turned in my resignation, I felt the weight of the world drop off my shoulders like a lead balloon falling off the edge of a cliff. It was a weight I so furiously held on to because of the fear of the unknown, the fear of success, and the fear of failure. I grew up with the mentality that I needed to go to work even if I was sick and that I couldn't quit my job unless I had another lined up and it was signed, sealed, and delivered. By resigning, I completely blew both of those rules that my mom and dad instilled in me.

I handed over my resignation paperwork, and before even looking at it, my boss asked me curiously if I was sure. I wasn't sure what was next, but I was confident that I never wanted to enter that building ever again. Instead of feeling guilty, I felt this whoosh of relief and the freedom of discovery when I told him that I was sure, and I walked out of the building without any regrets, knowing I had a lot of work ahead of me.

I hadn't been happy in years until that moment. It wasn't necessarily the workplace's fault, but more so what was in my own heart. If it doesn't feel right, no matter how much you try to fit in, you will only end up twisting your own shape. The quitting part was another prescription for my healing. Although I know not everyone can fill that prescription, for me it was a matter of life or death to make myself healthier in mind, body, and spirit. It was a true wake-up call. It was a lesson that an empath doesn't always learn in this lifetime.

Shifting my perspective was not just exhausting, it was enlightening. I realized I was resisting my destiny by staying in a job that didn't fit me, and that resistance was creating roadblocks in my life. I learned how to walk with the thoughts of my heart and look for the signs that speak so loudly at times; sometimes we ignore these signs because there's no rationality. It wasn't easy, but that day I opened myself up to what some may call the impossible and ridiculous. So, when I had the impulsive feeling to quit my very safe job to open an intuitive life coaching career, my family looked at me like they had never really known me.

In the past I had played it safe, but safe wasn't fulfilling me. I was playing dodgem cars with my own intuition. I finally embraced my intuitive calling and stopped calling the empath quality a curse. You read that right: I thought everything to do with being an empath was a curse. Up until that point, I felt like I was wearing a costume, all the while wanting everybody to see me for who I really was, and that ends up being confusing for everyone. It's a common empath trait to say, "It's okay that you don't see me for me," all the while screaming inside, "Why aren't you seeing me?!" If humans weren't already complicated enough, add in the empath trait.

If you are going through change, know that not everyone will be on board. That's okay, because it's *your* journey—not theirs. Your growth forces others to think that they need to grow too, and that can be scary for them. Stop worrying about what other people think of your choices and be you. Do you. Shine, bloom, and focus forward.

A GHOST OF AN ILLNESS

I was born an intuitive and an empath. I was also born being able to see spirits and communicate with them with all my senses. I see them. I hear them. I feel them. I can sense when they are around. I can smell and taste using my sixth sense along with all the normal senses. I was also born and raised in a haunted house. And they were not friendly ghosts, either. I had scary and dark experiences with scary and dark entities that challenged my thoughts of what life, death, and everything in between entailed. Because of my paranormal experiences growing up, I've made it a mission of sorts to help others who are having paranormal experiences. Anyone can learn by reading books and watching videos, but the real learning, training, and experiencing is by doing the work in the workplace. I've found that I learn something new about myself and the paranormal each time I visit an alleged haunted location. I use many of the tools I offer you in this book as means to protect and heal myself, but there are different levels to energy in both the living and the nonliving, and we aren't always as prepared as we might think.

One weekend, I had spent a few days investigating an old tuberculosis hospital with several paranormal investigation teams. When I meet new people, I can read the energy of a person before they utter a word, and this tells if they are a good person or not—or, at least, if they align with my energy. If we didn't align, it didn't mean that individual was a bad person, it just took some time for me to warm up or decide to move along. This team of people I was investigating the hospital with had all sorts of energy levels, and I felt overwhelmed.

To some members of the investigation teams, I may have come across as snooty. When I was a kid, I heard others call me all sorts of things: loner, shy, weird, snooty, stuck up. The truth was, I was a loner. I was shy. I was weird. And those things might make some people think I was snooty and stuck up, but I didn't think I was. I liked to hang around familiar or comfortable energies. And I felt the same way while investigating.

For my own energy preservation, I decided to stick with a group of familiar people so that I didn't have to prove myself in one way or another. I'd investigated with some of them before, and I knew they weren't using drugs and alcohol like other team members had that night. (People under the influence are kryptonite for me; being around them makes me under the influence without even touching any substance.) But then things were switched up and I found myself in a group of unfamiliar people. As we walked into one room of the old tuberculosis hospital, I felt as if I had been punched in the chest. I couldn't breathe. I thought perhaps I was having a heart attack.

"This area," our guide whispered, "was where they held experimental surgeries for those with tuberculosis. It was brutal. They'd take a rib from one patient and insert it into another. Or they'd do a lobotomy, or…"

"They were playing Frankenstein," I said flatly. "Is there a place I might be able to rest for just a minute? The energy is a bit much for me," I explained, almost embarrassingly.

Even in the dark, I could see some in the group roll their eyes at me. Okay, maybe I could just sense it. *Kristy's being melodramatic. She's making it about her.* I really wasn't trying to be dramatic, though—but it wasn't the first time anyone had thought that, and it certainly wouldn't be the last. I had to stick to my guns about how much energy I could take, and if that made me look like a diva, oh well. (Okay, not "oh well" at all. It still hurt my feelings that not everyone understood my intentions, but oh well. Okay, not "oh well," but you get the point.)

Another guide walked me to a different room where there was a chair. I sat down and tried to ground myself.

"Here." A woman kneeled beside me, pointing to the center of her chest where I had felt the pain. "You felt it right here, didn't you? I did too, but I didn't want to come across as high-maintenance—or, you know, *that* person."

I understood. Boy, did I understand. I wanted to tell her we empaths needed to stick together, but it wasn't the time or place.

"Do you know how to protect yourself and ground yourself?" I asked the woman. "I did it before we started, but sometimes the energy is so intense it can seep into any small hole in the energy field. Wait, that sounds very *Star Trek*-y," I laughed.

The woman laughed too, and I instantly felt the heaviness trickle away from both of us.

"Wait, how did that...?" She trailed off.

Laughter is high-vibrational energy, and it cleansed the icky energy immediately—at least for that moment. I was ready to return to the rest of the group.

The rest of the investigation was intense, and we had interesting experiences. (I'm not a fan of using the word *evidence* in a paranormal investigation because the paranormal isn't necessarily a science, nor is it a trial in a courtroom.) One of the experiences included a creepy-crawly shadow that slunk up the wall and on to the ceiling and then simply vanished. There was also a phantom energy that kicked my husband, Chuck, in the kidneys, making him ball up and roll around on the ground. He had to be carried down two flights of steps to the lobby to rest.

Chuck went to the hospital the next day and was diagnosed with bruised kidneys. The doctor asked, "How did you bruise your kidneys?" It was the million-dollar question, because "A ghost did it" didn't necessarily bode well in an emergency room, and that answer might have earned him a nice visit to the mental hospital.

It wasn't until a few days after the investigation that I started to feel incredibly ill. I couldn't breathe, I was coughing, my stomach hurt, and I had a high fever and night sweats. These symptoms lasted for a couple weeks. I could only take shallow breaths; if I tried to breath deeper, it hurt. I didn't have an appetite, and if I did eat, I coughed so hard I vomited. Then there was the low-grade fever that just didn't go away. It was exhausting. After a couple weeks I finally made an appointment with my physician, and thankfully, my doctor knows about my profession and my weirdness.

"It's weird," my doctor said after my examination, "your symptoms all signal tuberculosis, which is rare, but I think I'm going to give you a TB test."

"Tuberculosis?" I asked in between coughs. "I had a paranormal investigation at an old tuberculosis hospital a few weeks ago. Could that be why?"

The doctor smacked the palm of his hand on his forehead. "Tuberculosis." He shook his head in disbelief. I was either frustrating him or intriguing him. Or both.

"Well, I will give you a TB test. But could you have possibly picked up...What do you call them?"

"I call them hitchhikers. It might not be an actual ghost, but just the empath energy that is leftover. And it could possibly be that."

"Or your symptoms could be from investigating in a dusty old building filled with asbestos, animal droppings, and who else knows what. That could've given you an infection," my doctor suggested.

The buildings I investigate often *are* dusty and filled with asbestos, animal droppings, and who knows what else. Oh, and ghosts. There are plenty of ghosts. And in this case, there were plenty of ghosts who had died from tuberculosis.

My doctor wrapped up the appointment by saying, "So, go home and do whatever ritual you need to do to rid yourself of any hitchhikers. I'll run the tests, and come see me again in a few days. We will put you on a round of steroids then. Sound like a plan?"

I was pretty lucky to have a doctor who thought pragmatically—and who didn't think I should be committed to a mental institution.

I went throughout a gambit of tests, all of which came back clear. Nothing to explain my symptoms. Next, I did some holistic therapies like massage, reflexology, and smoke cleansing. And wouldn't you know it, I felt fine! Now, some people might say the germ just worked itself out of my system with time, but I don't think that is what happened. I believe I was sick because I am a physical empath. A physical empath who hasn't created healthy boundaries will find themselves vulnerable to both humans and spirits. It's happened many times to me, so this time around, I knew exactly why I wasn't feeling well.

Once, not having healthy boundaries landed me in the hospital with a migraine that just wouldn't go away. I had been invited to a home to do readings for several family members. One session was with a man who was a skeptic. At the urging of his wife, he sat across from me, and his grandfather came through immediately. As soon as his grandfather came through, the pounding in my neck and the back of my head began.

I knew the pain in my head had to do with the man's grandfather. Did he pass from a stroke? No. An aneurysm? Nope. The man's grandfather showed me his sad ending: He had been involved in a rollover tractor accident that decapitated him.

I told the man the messages his grandfather shared, but the pain was so intense that I had to excuse myself. I ended all my sessions and went to the emergency room. This time I had taken on a real and true migraine that required medication, although I did not tell my doctors that the migraine was a gift from a spirit who had a sad ending. In this instance, I think I so desperately wanted to make the nonbeliever a believer that I fully opened myself to spirit and discovered what a bad idea that was.

Don't get me wrong, I've left myself open before. Like I told the woman at the tuberculosis hospital, I always do a protection exercise before an investigation or before visiting a energetically high place, including grocery stores, retail shops, and malls. But even leaving a pin-sized hole in your own energy can be enough space for something to invade. That energetic hole might be caused by an argument, lack of sleep, worry, stress, or anything low-vibrational that leaves room for an energy stealer.

That was likely the case the time I got shot. (Not shot in a literal sense, but it sure felt like I was shot. And then stabbed by a sword.)

My husband and I were visiting Gettysburg when we found ourselves standing in the middle of the nineteen acres called the Wheat Field. The cool autumn sun was hidden behind an overcast sky where more than 6,000 men were killed, wounded, or captured. It was mid-October—not ideal tourist season—so we found ourselves alone. Or so we thought.

I began to take photographs, walking slowly through the field. As I walked, I suddenly felt as if I had been shot in the stomach. I fell to the ground. The pain was intense, and I wondered if it was caused by injury or empathy. I balled myself up on the sacred land. My moans surprised Chuck, who ran over to me.

"What's wrong?"

"I've been shot," I answered with surprise. "I've been shot!" I repeated, rolling around on the ground.

"Get in the car, Kristy!" he said, panicking. "Kristy, get up and get in the car now."

I sat up but still held my stomach. *Maybe this is something more than physical empath energy*, I thought, but then I discounted that because I could feel the blood coming out of my phantom wound.

"No, this is so cool. Who can say that they've been shot and not really have been sh—?"

Before I could finish my sentence, I heard the quick steps of a horse coming up to me and then felt a stabbing sensation underneath my right arm, as if someone had spiked me with a sword. "Now I've been stabbed," I said, falling back on the ground. "I'm dying." I wanted to laugh, but it hurt. Bad.

Chuck mumbled some swear words, picked me up off the field, and began to carry me to the car.

"Stop. Stop," I protested, "I'm okay. Honest."

"Get in the damn car, Kristy," Chuck argued, placing me in the passenger seat.

I visualized a rainfall of white light around me, washing away all the excess energy. After a few minutes, I began to feel the tension in my stomach release and the pain in my arm diminish. Chuck didn't say anything, just shook his head at me and then started to laugh.

"Honestly, Kristy."

I grinned back at him. "But how cool is it that I can say I was shot in Gettysburg?"

You would think I'd learn, right? *Right?* I don't know if it's my stubbornness or my determination to test every angle of being a physical empath. I mean, what could go wrong if I lay on a slab of concrete and was pushed into a crypt? Or if I was left alone in the death tunnels where more than 6,000 bodies were pushed down, nobody to ever come back up? Or if, at 3:00 a.m., I sat alone in a prison tunnel where prisoners were unfairly punished, some until they were beat to death? Why would I do any of that? Part of it was curiosity and part of it was training. I wanted to see how much I could endure, but I also wanted to learn the best way to cleanse myself after each scenario.

After sharing these crazy stories, I'm reminded of one of my favorite quotes: "We need the tonic of wildness...At the same time that we are earnest to explore and learn all things, we require that all things be mysterious and unexplorable, that land and sea be infinitely wild, unsurveyed and unfathomed by us because unfathomable. We can never have enough of Nature."[1] To find new oceans, we sometimes have to lose sight of the shore through wild exploration. Although there are negatives to being a physical empath, there are great positives to it too.

MISSING AND MURDER

For years, I've assisted the police on cases—especially cold and unsolved cases—by sharing information I get from the deceased. When I took the plunge and decided to call my gift a gift instead of a curse, I found myself working with police departments. At first,

....
1. Thoreau, *Walden and Other Writings*, 354.

I only worked with local departments, and then word got around and I started working with law enforcement agencies around the United States. I even worked with some private investigators. I was a psychic renegade and I had intentions to save everyone, find all the missing people, and point out the criminals to the police.

Once I started working with the police, I quickly realized that I didn't have superpowers and that the gift I did have wasn't well received by everyone. I also realized that I couldn't save everyone, unfortunately. It was an awakening that stung, and it still does, especially because I receive so many calls about missing people. Sometimes the calls come from family members of the missing, and sometimes they come from complete strangers who just want to see a cold case get solved. Think of the old show *Bewitched*; many people think I can just snap my fingers, wiggle my nose, and point to the location of a missing person on a map. It doesn't work that way.

One day, I received a phone call from a local sheriff. The very next day, I found myself sitting in a large conference room that doubled as a law library, with shelves of large books decorating three of the four walls. The other wall was covered in filing cabinets. In the center of the room was a wooden conference table and a dozen or so chairs, where I sat with the sheriff and several officers.

This case was different than most of the cases I assisted with. It involved a man who had simply disappeared. He was last seen on a frozen lake.

The sheriff began, "As I told you on the phone, Kristy, the family has asked for your help. They believe Matthew found himself in a precarious situation, and they'd like you to see if you can contact your angels and tell us more."

I nodded with understanding, but I had a problem. I could sense Matthew in the room, which meant he was deceased. His family had hired me for hope, and I was about to give them the opposite.

I could physically feel the water in my lungs, and I began to cough as if I had swallowed water that went down the wrong pipe. I couldn't stop coughing, and all the officers were staring at me as I sputtered out a request to point me toward the restroom.

In the bathroom, I threw up. I wasn't sure if it was nerves, the physical empath effects I was feeling, or the information I had to share. It was probably all of the above. I was still having a hard time taking a deep breath, but I found my way through the maze of cubicles back to the conference room.

After I sat back down, one of the officers next to me said, "Uh, Kristy. Before we start on Matthew's case, we were wondering if we could give you a couple more files. Some are solved. Some unsolved. We'd like to see what you get from them."

It was a nice way for them to tell me they wanted to test me. I was okay with being tested, but Matthew's presence was so overwhelming that I wasn't sure if I could turn him off and turn the other cases on. I worked so hard to protect myself, and now I was going to have to open myself up when I was already having a tough time. But I thought, *Oh, why not? What could go wrong?*

I nodded at the officer.

"Do you want a picture or a personal item?"

I shook my head. "No, just the sealed file in an envelope and a first name will work."

I smiled at each of the law enforcement officers. There were about seven of them, all standing around the table as if waiting for me to show them how a magic trick worked.

Someone handed me the first envelope. "Margaret or Margie," I was told by the detective.

I immediately smelled fire. I heard a scream. It was her scream that became my scream. I hated channeling, but the officers were asking for me to use everything I had, which included all my physical senses. I tasted blood in my mouth. I could feel blood rushing down my neck. The smoke was overpowering. I was dying, but what hurt the most was the betrayal by the man I loved the most: my husband.

I looked up at the sheriff and handed back the envelope. "The fire wasn't an accident. She was stabbed, almost to death, and then her husband started the fire to finish the job. Her life insurance and the insurance from the fire would help him and his mistress start a brand-new life."

The officers were all nodding in unison. Obviously, it was an already solved case. I took a sip of water and some deep breaths before reaching out my hand for another envelope, but the sheriff waved me away.

"You proved yourself, Kristy. We won't tire you any longer. I can tell this takes a toll, and we haven't even begun to deal with Matthew's case. I had no idea."

I was grateful for the validation of the exhaustion I felt because Matthew's case was also going to be rough. I felt his body under water. I could feel the ice on top of me as he tried hard to escape. Unfortunately, he couldn't find the hole he fell in.

Prior to Matthew's case, I'd never pointed out a resting place in water. With the currents, weeds, and weather conditions, I felt he was caught in the brush until a current moved him. I felt that current came from the ice being broken up by the police department so that they could do a search of the lake. Obviously, the sheriff thought he was in the lake too, as he had searched the lake several times before bringing me on.

We wrapped ourselves up in our warmest clothes and, with a diver and a K-9 unit, the department searched the lake. Sadly, I couldn't point to the location of Matthew's body. It took weeks for me to stop smelling fire from Margie's case, and it wasn't until months later that I felt warmed up from Matthew's case. It took about that long for spring to arrive and for his body to float.

I was using my gift for good, but I was also making some really bad mistakes. Not in my impressions or the information I was given, but in the way that I was going about things, especially the lack of protecting my body, mind, and soul. I have learned a lot since then. Now, I've taught myself not to feel the victim's pain as much. Instead, I sense or see their pain. I ask my guides and angels to show me what happened as if I was watching a movie rather than being the main character in the movie. By shifting or transferring the pain to something that you can view, you get a greater awareness. Sometimes the energy you are feeling isn't yours at all.

Move It to the Movie Theater

If you are feeling an overwhelming amount of energy, close your eyes and visualize a movie screen in front of you. Ask for the main character to appear on screen. Is it you? Or is it someone else? Ask for the area of pain to be lit up on the character in front of you, like an aura of sorts. You could ask for red to be physical pain and blue to be emotional pain. Keep in mind that pain is pain, no matter what you call it. Ask the main character to give you cues on how to heal that pain, or how to transfer that pain so you aren't carrying it. You could ask them to show a large piece of rock, name it PAIN, and ask them to destroy it. You could also ask them to simply offer tools to assist in the here and now.

You Have to Go ... Now

I'm really grateful to have such amazing clientele. Many of my clients have to book a year out for their appointment. One of my clients, Tanya, had booked her appointment a little over a year prior. She was giddy when I greeted her in my waiting room.

I invited Tanya in, gave her a water, and took her coat and hung it up. We sat down and began some small talk. Suddenly, I felt like I couldn't breathe. My stomach felt like it was being wrung over and over. Tanya looked at me, eyes wide. Unsure what to do, she just stared.

The wave of pain left me as soon as it came. I took a deep breath and tried to begin again, but the labor pain started all over again. When this wave ended, I stood up, handed Tanya her coat, and muttered wildly, "You have to go home. Your daughter is in trouble. Please, go. But don't stop anywhere, just go."

Tanya obviously thought I'd lost my mind. She said, "I can just call…"

I cut her off by vehemently shaking my head no and gently nudged her out the door. "No, go to her now. Don't stop anywhere. Go home."

Tanya gave me a hard look before heading to her car, but she left. I had no idea what I was feeling or why this was urgent, but as soon as Tanya left, my physical pain went away, although I was worn out.

That evening Tanya called me.

"Kristy, I don't know what to say. I left and immediately went home only to find my daughter balled up in her bed, in pain like you were having. I rushed her to the hospital. I won't go into all the sordid details, but she was pregnant, and we didn't even know it. She said she also didn't know it, but that is another story for another day. The doctors said she and the baby would've likely died if we hadn't gotten there as soon as we did. My daughter is recuperating, and my new granddaughter is in the NICU but will be fine. Thank you. Oh, and do I have to wait another year to come see you?"

I was relieved they were okay, and of course I didn't make her wait another year for her appointment.

I've had several of these types of occurrences. Once, a client sat down and I rushed her out of the session because I felt her husband was having a heart attack. He was. I also knew my husband had cancer even though all his tests came back normal. He had cancer, and we caught it early. Even if it doesn't make sense in the moment, trust your gift. But just know, you don't always have to feel your gift in ways that make you suffer.

USING YOUR PHYSICAL EMPATHY

Being a physical empath is a gift, sometimes classified under the psychic gift of *clairsentience*, or clear feeling. But how can feeling pain be a good thing? The pain is not for you or anyone else to suffer, it is for you as a physical empath to help heal at the core and not just at the root.

You don't have to call yourself psychic to make your gift a gift, though. There are several types of jobs where you could use your physical empath gift. Physical empaths might be:

- **Medical professionals** who can hone in on a problem even if science might be dissuading them away.
- **Spiritual healers** who sense physical anomalies in their client's energy.
- **Law enforcement officers or judges** who can feel that something is wrong with a case or person and dig further.

- **Teachers** who have suspicions that something is going on in a child's life without being told.

- A **parent or child caregiver** who can tune in to their child's needs.

- A **counselor or minister** who feels something else is going on with the person who sought out their services.

- **Creative individuals** who can physically feel their work flow through them.

TOOLS FOR A PHYSICAL EMPATH

There are many steps that a physical empath can take to be as healthy and happy as possible. I've included some suggestions for essential oils, crystals, and affirmations, as well as tips and a meditation for physical empaths.

MANIFEST HEALTH AND JOY

Most physical empaths are also emotional empaths, so if you are surrounded by people who are joyful, you will mirror those emotions and feelings no matter what's happening in your own life. The same goes for being around those who are depressed and crying. And, similarly, if you are around people who are ill in any way, you might experience the same symptoms.

Manifesting other people's symptoms is a common issue for physical empaths. The best thing you can do is surround yourself with healthy and happy people. Learn how to protect yourself so that you can properly cope, create healthy boundaries, keep your own stress to a minimum, and take care of you.

Pay attention to shifts in atmosphere and energy levels when you encounter other people. Does your mood lift or sink? Do you experience physical sensations? Does your head pound or heart swell? Do you feel a pit in your stomach? Do you feel like you can't breathe? Do random thoughts about the other person flow to you? Not every experience will be the same, but there might be similarities, so awareness is key to understanding your triggers.

MEDITATION EXERCISE FOR A PHYSICAL EMPATH

1. Close your eyes and take three deep breaths in and out.
2. Invoke the name of an ascended master/spirit guide/archangel of choice, then take in another deep breath.
3. Working with your ascended master/spirit guide/archangel of choice, set a specific intention to either shut down, reduce, or mute the volume of empathy.
4. Take several short breaths.
5. Thank your ascended master/spirit guide/archangel of choice.

When shutting off empathy, everything gets a lot quieter. This may feel unusual at first.

You can also use this meditation to turn empathy back on or to change the volume of empathy. It is merely conscious intention.

PROTECTION TIPS FOR A PHYSICAL EMPATH

- Ask the angels and guides (or whomever you pray to) to always keep a white bubble of protective light around you. This bubble is a protective shield that covers your aura. White light encompasses keep negative energy outside your bubble. You can still observe what is happening around you, but this helps so you don't absorb that energy. You can also create your own white light shield. Imagine that every time you inhale, you are breathing in a swirl of white light. As you exhale, that light wraps around your body, inside and out, and settles down by your feet. This light is the source of your protective shield. You can imagine it as a cloak, a bubble, or even an astronaut-like suit.

- Understand that spending time with people who complain about physical maladies might drain and deplete you. If you know you will be around a person who does this, reinforce your bubble.

- Cleanse your energy with smoke. Use white sage or palo santo once a week or after any interaction with a draining person. Don't forget to get the bottoms of your feet!

- Carry protective gemstones in your pocket or purse, or keep them on your desk.

- Utilize positive affirmations or mantras to keep you focused.

- Healers need healers, so make sure to seek out Reiki, massage, acupuncture, or anything else that resonates with you.

- Exercise. Movement also helps move along negative energy.

- Drink water to help release negative energy.

- Eat foods from the earth. This helps to ground you.

- Seek out a means to purge negative energy, perhaps by visiting a therapist, talking to a minister, or journaling.

ESSENTIAL OILS FOR A PHYSICAL EMPATH

Never use essential oils directly on the skin. Always dilute essential oils with a carrier oil like almond oil, grapeseed oil, coconut oil, or olive oil. Essential oils are incredibly concentrated. A few drops are generally all that is needed. Practice aromatherapy by diffusing essential oils or sprinkling a few drops on a handkerchief or pillow.

- **Ylang-Ylang:** Ylang-ylang can be an overpowering oil, so use it sparingly. It is an amazing oil that creates a relaxing atmosphere.

CRYSTALS FOR A PHYSICAL EMPATH

Empaths are sensitive and very intuitive. Because of this, the empath absorbs both positive and negative energies from other people and their surroundings. Empaths naturally want to take care of people, and they often become drained in body, mind, and soul as a result. Crystals are an amazing tool to help. The best crystals for empaths protect the energy field (sometimes called an aura), shield an empath from negative emotions, and keep the empath grounded. You can wear these crystals as a piece of jewelry, put them in your purse or pocket, or lay them near you.

- **Black Obsidian:** Black obsidian has protective energy that is helpful to empaths. It keeps unwanted negative energies at bay and provides a barrier so energy vampires cannot take advantage of the empath.
- **Hematite:** Hematite has a black or silver mirror-like appearance. It acts as a reflective shield to deflect unwanted energies and vibrations.

AFFIRMATIONS FOR A PHYSICAL EMPATH

- I have the power to clear all negativity and stress from my physical body.

- I embrace my wellness.

- I grow stronger in body, mind, and spirit every single day.

- I practice healthy habits.

- I trust the signals I receive from my body. They are communication from my intuition.

THREE
The Emotional Empath

ARE YOU AN EMOTIONAL EMPATH?

1. Have you ever been called oversensitive?

2. Do loud noises irritate you or cause you anxiety?

3. After spending time with someone, have you ever felt emotionally exhausted?

4. Do crowds make you feel tired, sick, or uneasy?

5. Do you tend to look out for the underdog?

6. Have you ever felt someone else's emotions in your own body, mind, or spirit?

7. Do you feel exhausted by angry people or feel the need to avoid them?

8. Are you chronically tired or suffering from depression or anxiety?

9. Do you feel as if you oversee everyone else's happiness?

10. Does seeing or hearing about a person or animal that is injured, sad, or going through a hard time emotionally hurt you?

If you answered yes to more than two of these questions, you are likely an emotional empath. You aren't crazy. You are simply someone with a gift that can be developed and better managed.

If you don't feel like you resonate with this trait, continue to read this chapter because it will help you understand someone in your circle who has this trait.

. . . .

Emotional empathy is an amazing way to connect with others, but an emotional empath doesn't just connect—they experience what another person is feeling. This isn't a bad thing if the emotion is joyful and happy, but it can be dangerous if the empath picks up negative, depressive, or sad traits. And if an emotional empath is around someone who is always in crisis mode, it can make an emotional empath feel nuts.

It's common for an emotional empath to not understand where their emotions come from. Is the emotion someone else's? Is it their own? This is because emotional empaths can feel emotional energy by being near people, by watching actors on television, and by the words expressed in books, music, songs, or status updates on social media.

LIFE AS AN EMOTIONAL EMPATH

Emotional empaths need to learn how to set healthy boundaries. From friends to family to random strangers at the hospital, emotional empaths will be asked to lend a listening ear.

BE A LIGHT

We aren't a one-size-fits-all world, and nobody else is you. Every emotional empath has different tolerance levels. Positive energy can never be forced. Positive change must be done with love, peace, kindness, and tolerance. Finding the positive in a stressful situation isn't easy—I get it—but through this change, we have the opportunity to compose a new vibration. If you are an emotional empath that complains and wallows in the negative energy that you pick up, you aren't helping yourself or others. You are only decreasing your vibration.

"I can't do social media anymore," my friend Aria moaned. "All this fighting. All this hate."

"Which is exactly why you need to stay on social media," I reasoned. "You need to be a spiritual gangster with the rest of us."

Aria lifted her eyebrow skeptically at me over FaceTime.

"Don't you get it? The darkness wants you to shrink. It wants you to hide. You forget you have the best weapon. This is your true purpose!"

"Okay, gang leader," Aria laughed. "I'll bite. What's my given weapon, Yoda?"

I responded with a giggle. "In a world of hate, we need light. We need *your* light. That is your weapon, but let me teach you something too. In your empath toolbox, you have the dimmer switch to how much you can handle right now. It's like a radio dial, but it controls how much light you want to emit into the Universe. All sorts of people are attracted to an empath's light. They sometimes want to abuse it. They sometimes want to bask in it for just a bit. Sometimes they want to steal it. Imagine stepping into a bubble of white light of protection, but with your dimmer switch, dim it. You are still protected with white light, but you have cloaked yourself. You are in control. If you see or sense someone that needs your light, you can turn that light up, but you are still protected."

I didn't want Aria to sacrifice herself by staying on social media if she truly didn't want to. But the thing is, empaths tend to run and hide when things get heavy in lieu of facing the situation head on. Sometimes that is best, but an emotional empath must also learn how to stand up for themselves. Emotional empaths must learn how to create proper boundaries, even on social media.

Aria decided to look at how much time she was spending online. For one week, she set a timer every time she went on social media. At the end of the week, she calculated her total and decided to finesse things. She went through her social media accounts and unfollowed and deleted people who just didn't serve her life objectives any longer. She removed herself from groups that she was no longer interested in, and she began to time herself online instead of jumping down the rabbit hole of endless scrolling. After a month, she felt lighter and filled with less negativity.

Sure, there's a lot of ugly out there, but there's a lot of good too. In fact, I believe there's more good than bad. Finding the good doesn't mean you have to sacrifice your mental state, but we all have choices. We have the choice to change the channel. We have choices to block, unfriend, hide, or just ignore. Not every disagreement needs to be an argument, and you don't have to show up for every fight you're invited to. You don't have to agree with everything, but by shining your light out, you might be helping someone. Anyone.

You might be the light in their storm. You may not even know how much help you are offering, but you are making a difference.

Life is about balance. It's so easy to get weighed down by the negative and sit in the darkness, wondering where the light is. It's easy to stay focused on the bad people and to allow that to tarnish you. The worldwide web is filled with people who gaslight, stonewall, devalue, and spew venom. So how do you allow your light to still shine without allowing the darkness to creep in?

- **Set boundaries.** Block. Ban. Unfriend. Like attracts like, so don't keep anyone around if they don't fit your objective.

- **Set an alarm.** Allot yourself so much time online per week.

- **Practice self-love.** Work on getting fit in body, mind, and spirit. The more you work on yourself, the more it will be obvious who belongs in your circle. When you grow, it might scare some people because it means they have to grow too, or it makes them feel bad for not growing. These are people you don't need in your life.

- **Ignore.** The quickest way to get rid of negative energy in your online content is to stop the conversation.

- **Limit your online time.** Get out in nature. Explore. Read a book. Do a puzzle.

- **Focus on love.** Fill your online feed with all things love.

Another way to focus on light is to ask your spiritual team for help. I often call on Archangel Michael, my guides, and Source (God/Universe, etc.) and ask for the brightest and most healing white light to pour on top of me. (I say white light, but you can use any color.) I visualize that light coming from the ceiling and washing over me, encasing me in the highest protection. Then, in my mind's eye, I visualize a dial and I dim the outer core of the white light. Think of it this way: You may be protected by the light you emit, but that light will attract anything and everything. This is why I use a dimmer, so that only those of the white light will find me, instead of those who want to suck the light from me.

MIND YOUR BUSINESS

Have you ever been minding your business in a store when someone comes up to you and tells you their life story or just randomly asks for advice? I've had strangers come up to me in the produce section of the supermarket and ask me if I have a good roast recipe. Since I do, I share it, but how did they know I'd have a good roast recipe? I've had strangers ask me to help them choose a dress for their friend's wedding. I mean, they don't know I have good taste. Most of the time I'm wearing jeans and a punny T-shirt; I don't wear a shirt that reads "Ask me anything!" And it's not my looks. I can be wearing a face mask, a baseball hat, and sunglasses, yet someone will still come up to me and ask if they should buy the sandalwood scented candle or the strawberry scented candle. They know I can help them because of the energy I exude. In their mind's eye, that person who came up to you felt or saw your light. Sometimes this might not be a big deal, but some days you might not want to deal with it. We are all given that dimmer switch to create boundaries, and it's up to us to enforce them.

It was January of 2021 when my husband had a heart procedure for atrial flutter. Just a few months before, Chuck had a stem cell transplant for multiple myeloma. The atrial flutter was a fun gift from chemotherapy. The stem cell transplant is a beautiful science where they take stem cells, clean them up, and offer high doses of chemotherapy before giving the patient back their cleaned-up stem cells. After seven hours of surgery, the doctor came into the hallway looking grim. There'd been a complication. They'd nicked an artery. Instead of going home that day, Chuck was being admitted.

I was beside myself. My intuition had a bad feeling as soon as the procedure was scheduled, but I didn't want to be a major manifester either. Although there were sleepless nights of wondering how to proceed with the intuitive nudge, I was keeping things dorky, the way I almost always try to when things are heavy. I didn't want my family to know I was worrying, so on the way to the hospital I was telling Chuck jokes, singing fun songs really loud (he especially loves when I do that), and keeping it easy breezy—all the while intuitively knowing that something was going to happen.

Thankfully, this was a minor setback, but I was still emotional. So, there I was, sitting in the hallway of the hospital with a face mask on, a coat on, sweatpants on, wearing two pairs of socks, and with three heated blankets wrapped around me. I was both cold because it *was* cold and cold because I was cloaked with a deep sadness. (For some reason, I get cold when I'm sad.) I had work laid out on the table in front of me, but I started calling our kids to let them know the news. In between doctors and nurses filling me in with more information and navigating between texts and calls from our four kids, a twenty-something-year-old man came up to me.

"I hope you're ready," he said, standing maybe four feet away, his face mask sitting below his nose. "It's about to get challenging here in this world, and you need to be ready. Food, water, even ammo. You got it all, right?" he pressed.

I smiled at him, nodded, and said, "I'm all good." I held up my phone, gesturing that I had to make a phone call, but he didn't take the hint. Instead, he got closer to me and pulled off his mask.

"I'm not kidding. I just had a baby girl and I'm not letting her grow up in a communist country. I will enter this civil war for her."

Half of me wanted to bolt and find security, but my empath gift told me I needed to talk to him. I read between the lines of his words. He was scared. He was a new daddy. He was afraid she wouldn't be proud of him. He wanted to be a hero. He wasn't happy with who he was to begin with. He wanted to feel important. It's why he was letting a complete stranger know they needed to prep.

I said, "Sir, this world is scary. Every generation has had fears of war. Please don't do anything you'll regret that might lead to you not being around for your daughter."

The man scoffed at me. "I am not going to hide. I need to be vigilant, just like you do."

"I'm not telling you to hide, I am telling you to be—"

"Smart." The man finished my sentence.

"Yes. Be smart. This isn't the Wild West."

"There's a quote by Winston Churchill that says, 'Mountaintops inspire leaders, but valleys mature them.' I am going to climb the mountaintop!"

"The valley isn't a bad place to be either," I reasoned with him, using his own quote. "There's also a saying that you can no more win a war than you can win an earthquake. The more you find peace within yourself, for yourself and for your daughter, the better you can soldier through this without major combat."

He nodded at me in deep thought, pulled his face mask back up over nose, and pivoted like a soldier toward the hallway. "Thanks for the talk. I have some thinking to do."

"You'll be a good daddy. Now, go hug and kiss on your daughter," I called out to him.

As if on cue, my phone rang. I waved a goodbye and answered the call.

Boundaries are important. I didn't really force him to follow any of mine, but sometimes an empath needs to be an empath. Sometimes a healer needs to heal.

THE BOUNDARY BUBBLE

It's hard to keep boundaries in a 24/7 world, especially for an emotional empath. Everyone wants an immediate response, whether that is via text, email, or phone call (although those are rare, right?), and an empath aims to please. In the past, I too have complained, "They always have their phone in their hand. Why aren't they answering me?"

I, for one, was tired of the phone in the hand. Isn't it funny that we were more connected by being *less* connected before cell phones? In early 2020, my husband and two of our adult kids and their spouses decided to take a quick four-day adventure to the happiest place on earth, Disney World. (This was pre-COVID.) This trip was a celebration in many ways—mostly that we had survived 2019, as it had been stressful with the death of my husband's mom. On top of that, neither of our kids got to have a honeymoon due to military training. We wanted to give them some time away (albeit with their parents tagging along). No laptops allowed. Phones set to emergency calls/texts only. We were going to create boundaries from real life. Or so that was the plan. And the plan succeeded—until I started to receive several messages that began "I know you're on vacation, but..."

I've always been a people pleaser, but then I added a business to my resume and it got even worse. Owning my own business made me feel like I needed to always be available to my clients and customers, but at what sacrifice? On the first evening of our vacation, I sat on the bus headed back to our resort and started to cry. I was at the happiest place on earth, but I was feeling overwhelmed.

If I didn't answer my client, she would hate me, or leave me a bad Yelp review, or tell all her friends I was terrible and that I didn't answer. Or she'd never book another appointment. Or she'd unfriend me. And then I stopped my down-the-rabbit-hole thinking and thought about how ridiculous I was being. If anyone hated me, they didn't really know me. It was up to me to set my boundaries.

So I did. I explained that I was on vacation, as she knew, and that I was trying to avoid any work. There was absolutely no drama. The client understood. I had reacted too emotionally to the situation. But there were several reasons why I did that other than being a people pleaser; I was also overstimulated by the crowds at the parks that day, and I was still tired from traveling.

Emotional empaths are notorious for allowing others to break our bubble of boundaries. We can complain about boundaries being crossed, but we must remember to set them and to continue creating reinforcement. Those who genuinely love you will want you to do what's best for you when it comes to self-care, which is not selfish. Those who genuinely love you may not like the boundaries you set, but they will respect them.

Do you have habits that are draining you, disintegrating your boundaries, or stressing you out? I realized on my vacation that I needed to make changes in my life. That included closing my laptop and silencing my phone at a decent time of night and not turning my electronics back on until 8 a.m. (I receive texts and calls at all hours of the night from clients or potential clients.) I learned that I need to take days off and not just *say* they are days off—I truly need to not work on those days. I also needed to stop saying yes when I wanted to say no. I needed to stop apologizing, which sometimes sounded like excuses. I also had to be more attentive to my own energy levels so that I didn't defensively react or overreact, because jumping down Alice in Wonderland's rabbit hole is cute when you're at Disney, but not when it's in your own mind.

Life is short. Tomorrow isn't guaranteed. Make your time well spent and treat yourself well. Boundaries aren't easy, but they are needed. Repeat after me:

I don't have to do what everyone wants me to do.

I don't have to anticipate everyone's needs.

I don't need anyone to approve of me.

I don't have to explain myself.

I don't need to feel guilty for having boundaries.

I don't have to say yes if I want to say no.

I don't need to feel bad if I want to stay home.

I don't have to put others before myself.

I don't need to feel what others feel.

It is not my job to fix everyone (or anyone).

I don't have to overextend myself.

I am allowed to take time to relax.

I don't have to be connected to my computer/phone.

I don't have to immediately answer everyone.

I don't have to fight everyone to prove I'm right.

I am allowed to be kind to myself.

I am allowed to speak up for myself.

I am allowed to peacefully step away from situations.

I'm not saying go hide, but I am saying that we all have our unique vibration—our own lane, if you will. Sometimes people aren't happy with their own lane, and they will play Bumper Cars, especially when they meet an empath. They want to test you to see if you'll move out of your lane. In today's world, we have a lot of energy swerving around and we are losing our focus. We are forgetting where our lane is. We are spinning out of control, whether out of fear, anger, hate, jealousy, etc. Remember to gain control of *your* energy. Remember that you don't need to answer to anyone for why you are doing what you are doing, because that's your business.

I'M SORRY

An empath is sensitive to visible and invisible energy. An empath feels all the feelings around them and acts as an emotional sponge. Empaths are so emotionally connected to others that they experience the emotions of those around them as if they are their own. When an empath senses something is wrong or senses someone is in a bad mood, they often assume it is something they caused. They own another's person's issues, often apologizing for what isn't even theirs to apologize for.

An empath can be easily taken advantage of because of their good intentions, so pay attention to who your energy increases or decreases around. It is an indicator of who you should be around— or not. Now, everyone has a difficult day sometimes, but if a person's negative emotional energy is consistent, then that isn't a sign, it's a billboard. Claiming everyone else's luggage and carrying it around is exhausting. Set it down and make sure your luggage tag matches what you are picking up.

I used to take on things that were not my issue. This was a big problem of mine when I worked at one of my old jobs. It wasn't news to me nor my coworkers that my boss hated me. He was an impatient, fast talker, and I was a patient explainer. He discounted everything I said, did, or suggested. He was exhausting. I exhausted him as well. It was a toxic and infuriating work environment, but my boss taught me to shift out of a dangerous emotional empath trait: over apologizing.

I would walk into a room and say "I'm sorry" to whoever was there. My boss would hand me work to do, and I'd say "I'm sorry." I'd hand him his coffee with an "I'm sorry," or I'd let him know there was a phone call for him, and I would start the sentence with "I'm sorry."

After several years of working for him, my boss called me into his office and asked me to sit down. Of course, I thought I'd done something wrong. You know how you might get jittery when a police officer follows you in their car even though you know you were following all the rules? Well, when things get serious, an empath often immediately goes into the mind frame that they've disappointed the other person.

"Kristy, I like you," my boss started.

I'm fired. I'm sure I'm fired. I wanted to throw up.

"But there's something I need to talk to you about."

I'm suspended?

"You are a good person. You care about your work. You care about our customers and the employees. Heck, you even care about me, and I treat you like crap."

Wow, he noticed?

"But you have to stop apologizing. You apologize for *everything*. Unless you are terribly sorry because you did something wrong, I don't want to hear you say sorry."

I began to tear up. I wasn't sure if it was because I was relieved that I wasn't being fired or because I was sorry that he was upset I said sorry too much.

"Think of it this way. Every single time you walk into a room and apologize, you are apologizing for your presence because there's nothing you did that required an 'I'm sorry.' You are telling the Universe that you are worthless, and you aren't worthless. So, I'm asking—no, demanding—that you stop saying 'I'm sorry.' You can say 'pardon me' or 'excuse me,' but there will be no more 'I'm sorry.' Got it?"

I nodded and began an "I'm sorry," but I stopped myself at the "I'm" and just nodded.

"Good. Now clean up your face and get me those reports."

Our relationship never got better, but that boss helped me grow. I realized that when I stopped apologizing for things that didn't need to be apologized for, the end result was amazing. I felt more secure, confident, and worthy.

We are taught early on to have manners, and that includes learning to apologize. But an empath takes apologizing to the extreme. That one word—sorry—can be damaging to an empath because it negates their own feelings and their own self.

What Should You Stop Apologizing For?
- **Feeling your feelings.** We are all human, and nobody should apologize for feeling their emotions and expressing themselves.

- **Your appearance.** I've changed my hair color and haircut frequently, and it's often commented on. I get comments on my weight. Someone a few months ago told me they hated my eyeliner. Another told me to dress my age (whatever that means—I mean, my petticoat was being laundered). I notice, but instead of apologizing, I laugh.

- **Self-care.** I used to feel so guilty about taking an hour to get a massage or spending money on getting a manicure every so often. No matter what your self-care looks like, it is needed for your well-being; it isn't optional.

- **Another person's behavior.** How many times have you been embarrassed by someone else's behavior (a spouse, a boss, a coworker, a friend, etc.) and you apologized for them? Nope. It's not your responsibility. It's not yours to carry.

Are you a chronic apologizer like I was? Next time you feel like saying sorry, take a few deep breaths and see if it truly is a sorry that you need to say. If so, say it and mean it. Often, it's the other person's issue.

And if you feel bad but it's not your sorry to own, there are other things you can say: "Thanks for pointing that out." "Thanks for the feedback." "Maybe we should look at this differently." Or whatever the situation might be! Sometimes the situation requires no words at all.

KNOW YOUR VALUE

An emotional empath will often give up their value to make someone else feel worthy or simply to avoid causing a scene. Myself included.

I was at an event where I was speaking and selling my books. A lady came up to me, looked me up and down, looked over at my banner, and then looked back at me.

"If you are so great and you wrote all these books"—she waved her hands at my stack of books—"then why haven't I heard of you?"

"Well…" I began, my mouth gaping open and my defensiveness growing. I closed my mouth, took a deep breath, and began again. "It's about timing. Maybe the Universe didn't want you to know about me. Maybe we aren't vibrationally aligned."

"Hmph," she responded, looking at my books. "My name is Judith, by the way. Tell me about your process with your readings, and then I'd like to know your writing process. I just know I have a bestseller or two in here." She smacked her finger against her temple.

There was a lengthy line of people waiting to speak to me, and as much as I didn't want to be rude, I kept hearing *Know your value* in my head, so I handed Judith my business card. "My website speaks about all my services, and I offer a lot of different classes. As for writing, I just write. Not to create a bestseller—don't tell my publisher that—but because it's something inside me that has to come out."

Judith wasn't happy with that, and she asked the question again, this time more persistently. I still didn't give her the answer she wanted. Then she asked for a deal on my books because she'd "never heard of" me before.

"It was great to meet you," I smiled. "Maybe the Universe will align us in the future."

A lady who had been waiting patiently interrupted before Judith could try again. The woman picked up three of my books, handed me the correct change, and asked me if I'd sign them.

Judith left without purchasing anything, and I gave a huge sigh that resembled a released balloon. During that conversation with Judith, I had my husband and best friend sitting right next to me, and they had just stared.

"Hey, where were you? I could've used some help!" I smirked.

"You did just fine," they said in unison.

Judith didn't mean to be rude, I'm sure. She was just more assertive than the people I typically align with. We are often tested by people like Judith to see if we'll keep our value, whether that value is losing your patience, getting sucked into an argument on social media, or making you feel bad about yourself. You can be tested by someone you know, someone you love, or a total stranger.

When you stop knowing your value and start discounting who you are and your energy, you dip into a lower vibration that can create all kinds of problems. Have you ever read a text message or an email as something negative and responded defensively, only to realize you read it the wrong way? Every time that's done, you lose your value, and you have to save to get that vibrational value back up. I hope that if you ever have an interaction with a Judith, you will be secure in knowing your value. Keep your vibration right where it is so that you don't have to do the extra work of saving it back up.

Hurting Yourself While Helping Another

Emotional empaths can be assertive and still be true to themselves, but first, that requires recovering from being a people pleaser. Being a people pleaser means you stop pleasing yourself, and it ultimately doesn't help anyone. The struggle is real.

Many of us were raised to make others happy, whether that involved cleaning your plate, cleaning your room, staying out of trouble, being respectful to your elders, or anything in between. If you were raised this way and you made someone happy, you were a good boy or girl. You were taught to please the external world around you. If you didn't make someone happy with your choices or actions, then you were punished.

Well, an empath took that programming to the nth degree. Empaths were taught our boundaries weren't worthy. Empaths are often thought of as a doormat or a pushover. Some people even think empaths are weak. And the more we continue with these taught traits, the more the traits persist and are passed down to more generations. This is why it is crucial to set boundaries.

So, what is a healthy boundary? A boundary is a personal limitation that makes you feel comfortable. Everyone has their own personal boundaries based on their own beliefs, opinions, ethics, morals, values, and religion. Boundaries are not put in place to limit your happiness, but to protect it. Boundaries are not created to hurt anyone. Having boundaries does not make you oversensitive. You have the right to shift, change, and/or move the boundary according to your personal growth. You don't have to explain or defend your boundaries.

What does it look like when you can't create healthy boundaries?

- **You are surrounded by difficult people.** You have people in your life that don't care about your feelings. Talking to them is exhausting.

- **You are surrounded by drama.** You have relationships in your life that are fueled by drama and make you feel uncomfortable.

- **You stop trusting your decision-making.** You might be wishy-washy when it comes to making decisions.

- **You are fatigued.** You suffer emotional burnout or fatigue.

- **You lose yourself.** You put everyone else's needs before your own. You might even lose track of what your own needs are.

- **You are afraid to say no.** You are concerned that if you say no or create a boundary, you will sabotage your relationships.

- **You feel misunderstood.** Your relationships with others make you feel disconnected and disrespected.

- **You have unhealthy coping mechanisms.** You might smoke, use alcohol or drugs, or eat too much or too little.

- **The tables turn.** You might be accused of being passive-aggressive.

The solution is to be assertive. But when empaths hear that they should be assertive, it just feels wrong. It feels like someone is telling them to be rude. Assertiveness is *not* about being crass. Boundaries can be rooted in kindness and love. There are many benefits to being assertive, including:

- **Better Communication:** Being assertive allows you to express yourself more confidently. You're less likely to have misunderstandings.

- **Better Self-Esteem:** When you do something that feels right for you, it improves your self-esteem.

- **Better Relationships:** When you set boundaries, there's nothing you are hiding. You are being genuine, clear, and authentic. Healthier people will be drawn to you, and the unhealthy people will slink away.

- **Clearer Direction:** Not only will you have better direction for yourself, but you will also be able to help others with their direction.

- **Less Anxiety:** When you aren't busy feeling obligated to fix everyone else, you will be better grounded, which results in less anxiety and depression.

EMOTIONS ARE HEAVY

Emotional empaths go through life trying to carry everyone's emotional weight, forgetting that unless we talk about it or ask someone to help us, it just keeps getting heavier. And day by day, the load gets carried. Nobody knows what we need unless we tell them. If you don't ask for help, happiness won't be found in the next place you go. It's not at your next job or with your next partner. It's not a new coat or a bigger house. Happiness will never be where you are if you just stay preoccupied, hoping that someone else will figure out what you need. Often, *you* don't even know what you need until you start confronting it. It's like going to the doctor and saying "Guess!" when they ask what your symptoms are.

A heavy emotion to carry is pride. There is a saying that goes, "Stop trying to keep up with the Joneses. They are broke." Pride isn't necessarily about money or things; it's also about emotional pain. The more your pride tells you not to release the weight you are carrying—that you are strong and you've got it—the more cranky you get, and sometimes you don't even realize it.

I woke up cranky one morning. There really wasn't a good reason why I was cranky; I just was. As soon as I got off work, I wanted to just call it a night. But there were things to do, so I couldn't escape to my comfortable bed and mope for no reason. Instead, I stomped around the house being cranky.

I was also hungry, but I was in a standoff with my husband, who was completely unaware that we were fighting. The past three nights I had cooked dinner after getting off work, and even though we had both gone to the store to buy food for specific meals on specific dates, there he was, sitting on the couch playing a game on his phone.

The longer he sat there, the crankier I got.

I'm not cooking dinner again, I said to myself. *I'm tired. I'm cranky. I'm not doing it.*

But you see, I wasn't telling Chuck that and, well, he's not a mind reader. Although he is a good listener, he's actually not very good at taking hints. Being direct is best, and I could've just said, "Would you fix dinner tonight?" But no, instead I festered in an immature fashion.

An hour later, Chuck stood up, looked at me, and asked if he was supposed to cook dinner. So either someone texted him (I'm guessing one of our kids who was carefully watching the interaction) or he finally got the hint (doubtful).

But you know what I said in reply? "I think so," followed with, "It's fine. I'll just do it." Now, those might not be fighting words, but I think he heard the lilt in my voice because he got off the couch really quick and began to make dinner. It turned out amazing, and I told him so, and it seemed that part of my crankiness was hanger (hunger mixed with anger). And after dinner, Chuck sat down with me and asked me what was wrong. It seemed the other part of my crankiness was a weight I was carrying that I was afraid of unloading.

The next time I was cranky, I figured out healthy ways to help that didn't include stomping around and being passive-aggressive.

I cried.

I turned on music and danced around (without stomping).

I ate good food.

I drank water.

I listened to a positive podcast.

I took a sea salt bath with essential oils. (A shower would do the trick too.)

If you don't have a friend or partner that you can vent to, journaling your feelings helps. Therapy helps too.

A BALANCING ACT

When an emotional empath can balance their gift, still save space for their gift, and not allow their gift to overwhelm them, they find their sweet spot. It isn't easy, though. Emotional empaths are sensitive to television, news, and music. If they see anything violent or emotional—especially if it involves a child or animal—it can topple the empath off-balance. Empathy isn't bound by space or time, so there's unlimited opportunities for an empath to be bombarded or overloaded.

I called a friend one day to check up on her. I could tell she was crying, but she hadn't divulged any bad news.

"What's wrong?" I asked.

"It's so stupid. A commercial came on this morning and it pulled at my heartstrings and made me cry. Now I can't shake the images, and every time I think about it, I start to cry again."

Not stupid at all.

I had another friend who sobbed every time Christmas music came on. It didn't matter if it was "Jingle Bells" or the gut-wrenching "The Christmas Song."

For me personally, anytime I step into a church—even if it's one I'm touring or doing a paranormal investigation in (yes, that happens)—I start to cry.

An emotional empath often avoids things that cause them distress. They might turn off any commercials that deal with hurt animals or kids in need. It's not because they don't have feelings, it's because they feel so much. That's why emotional empaths are often drawn to healing professions. They want to try and fix everyone, which is both dangerous and admirable.

BECAUSE I DON'T WANNA

Empaths often sacrifice their own time and energy rather than speaking up. They strive to bring peace rather than cause conflict. However, that's self-sabotage and can cause an array of issues down the line. It's like sweeping dirt under the rug—eventually there will be a lump that you'll trip over and have to deal with it.

I share an office building with several other healers. Some are psychiatrists. Others are psychologists, social workers, nutritionists, Reiki therapists, or massage therapists. And then there's me, a psychic medium.

Aliza, one of the building's psychologists, was stomping around the office building all morning, but I was busy with clients and didn't have time to talk to her until that afternoon, when I had an hour between sessions. I was going to knock on her office door, but first I decided to make some hot chocolate in our little kitchen.

Aliza stormed in and slammed her "Happy Ho Ho Ho" coffee mug down on the counter. She filled it with hot water, adding sugar and cream to it. I attempted to stop her before she took a sip, but it was too late.

"Blech," she screeched, quickly pouring her cup's contents into the sink. "I wish people would stop—" She paused. "Oh yeah, I made tea for my first client and left the hot water on the burner," she said, mostly to herself. "Hot water?" she offered me.

I laughed at her quick recovery. I shook my head no and pointed to my hot chocolate in the microwave. I only make my hot chocolate with milk, not water. (Almond milk, if you need specifics.)

"What's on your mind, A?" I gently probed.

Aliza was an intelligent, educated woman who breezed in and out of her office with class and elegance. She always wore bright colors, flowing kimonos, and a wisp of hibiscus fragrance. She was an amazing therapist who emitted more confidence than I had in my right thumb. Nothing ever seemed to get to her, and yet today she was off.

"My husband Herb is making me go to his Christmas party," she said matter-of-factly. "And I don't wanna go."

"Oh," I replied, trying to figure out a line of questioning that didn't sound judgmental in nature.

Since quitting the corporate world almost two decades prior, I personally missed holiday parties. It's the reason why I added holiday events for my clients to my calendar and why I have several holiday parties for friends and family at my house. In essence, I love everything Hallmark, everything flannel, and everything Christmas. The decorations. The good food. The yummy drinks. The music. I can be a bit much.

"What is wrong with Herb's Christmas parties?" I said, deciding that was safe to ask.

Aliza sighed heavy and slumped into one of the leather armchairs we have sitting in the waiting room. She chomped on her bottom lip before answering, then whispered, "Everything. I hate the food. I don't drink and everybody does. I don't like loud places, and they have the music blasting, and someone is always trying to pull somebody up to embarrassingly sing karaoke. I have to be *on* the whole time. I have to pretend to be the perfect wife. The perfect person. I feel drained for days after. I just don't wanna go, but that leads to multiple other issues." Aliza looked at me. "Is that enough reasons?"

"Honestly, you don't need any reason to not want to go. 'Because I don't want to' is a good enough reason. When did we become a society filled with excuses, with more excuses for the excuses? Nobody is entitled to your energy unless you want to give it away. It is *your* choice."

"I don't want to hurt Herb, though."

That I understood. Emotional empaths are chronic people pleasers, though. Although being a people pleaser might not seem like a bad thing, it can cause a lot of problems that might not show up immediately. People pleasers love to feel needed, but eventually they might feel taken advantage of or as if their own needs are being neglected.

"Compromise then, maybe? Go for dinner and then leave. That way you miss the big party. Would Herb be okay with that? I mean, he loves you, and if you were physically injured and felt like you couldn't go, he'd understand. You are emotionally fragile in that space. Explain that to him."

Aliza talked to Herb. Herb knew she hated the parties but had no idea why. They stayed for dinner and Aliza relaxed because she knew they were going to leave after. She relaxed so much knowing there was an exit strategy that they stayed for some of the party, and Aliza didn't feel so overwhelmed by it.

Side note: Isn't it interesting that healers often don't take the advice they dish out to their clients?

What Is a People Pleaser?

Empaths are natural people pleasers. A people pleaser is someone who puts the needs of others above their own in order to make another person happy. It often comes at an expense of their own needs. People pleasers do not like anyone being angry with them and try to avoid conflict at all costs. They feel responsible for the emotions of others and tend to over-apologize. They may anticipate and try to meet the needs of someone before being asked. People pleasers believe it is their responsibility to make other people happy. People pleasers are also natural caregivers, whether a person needs to be cared for or not.

People pleasers can be so busy taking care of everyone else that they forget to take care of themselves. They identify so strongly with caregiving and agreeing with others that they can lose sight of their own needs, values, and beliefs. Their kindness and their difficulty saying no can lead to other people taking advantage of them. People pleasers can become overworked and overburdened. *Thinking you are a bad person for saying no is a symptom of the disease to please.*

Remember: "No" is a complete sentence. It's important to be there for those you love, but you don't have to be there for everyone. You don't have to be burdened or burnt out by other people's energy, whether it is negative energy or just too much energy.

EMPATH SIDE EFFECTS

Most empaths have peculiar side effects from their gift. Just as a physical empath may receive physical symptoms, an emotional empath receives emotional symptoms. It's often hard to decipher between what is real and what is energy.

Actors have even talked about receiving emotional trauma from certain roles, including actress Nicole Kidman, who has acted in several intense projects. Nicole Kidman explained that she "becomes" her character, and that her own personality takes a pause while the personality of her character and all the character's experiences become the truth of the moment. She also shared that she has become very ill during productions because her immune system can't tell the difference between acting and real life.[2]

Our bodies react to what our mind is seeing, thinking, and experiencing. Negativity circles us every single day, but how we handle it determines our own personal happiness. It's important for an empath to dump out negativity and extreme emotions, whether they are real, created, or made up. Otherwise, an empath might set themselves up for real and true physical issues.

Easier said than done.

In short, spending time with negative people, also called *drainers*, will rob you of your energy. Spend time with positive people, also considered *energizers*, and in positive situations, and you will absorb more of that positive energy. Drainers drain you. Energizers energize you.

TOOLS FOR AN EMOTIONAL EMPATH

There are many steps that an emotional empath can take to be as healthy and happy as possible. I've included some suggestions for essential oils, crystals, and affirmations, as well as tips and a meditation for emotional empaths.

....

2. Contreras, "Nicole Kidman Reveals the 'Disturbing' Side Effects She Endured from *The Undoing*."

SET YOUR ENERGY

I set my energy at the beginning of each day so that I can stay balanced.

Imagine a positive energy radiating from your heart center. It is flowing within your body, from head to toe. The positive energy disallows negative energy. If negative energy does enter your body, instead of absorbing it like a sponge, it flows out of you like a faucet for the angels to care for.

MEDITATION EXERCISE FOR AN EMOTIONAL EMPATH

1. Call upon Archangel Michael and Archangel Raphael. You can also call upon other archangels, ascended masters, etc.

2. Envision the angels vacuuming up residue of emotions around your body, mind, and spirit. These are emotions that you don't need or can't control, heal, or help. They may also be emotions that have been dropped at your feet by others.

3. As the angels vacuum, the energy is spun into the most beautiful light you've ever seen. That energy is then sent to the Divine to be cared for. The Divine will do whatever needs to be done. That energy does not own you, nor do you own it.

4. Check to see if you feel lighter or if more energy might need to be dumped and vacuumed. Repeat if necessary.

Remember, the angels have as much time as you need to help you feel healed.

PROTECTION EXERCISE FOR AN EMOTIONAL EMPATH

Mindfulness is an amazing protection tool for empaths. Mindfulness makes you aware of your thoughts and feelings. The more awareness you have, the better you are able to control it. Because an emotional empath wants to heal, this protection exercise doesn't just help the empath, it helps those an empath wants to help as well.

1. Sit or lie down in a comfortable place where you won't be disturbed.

2. Turn your lights down or shut them off entirely. You might want to turn on some calming music.

3. Now focus on yourself. Go inward. Breathe in. Breathe out. Does the breath feel panicky or steady? If it feels panicky, take a deep breath in and out again, like a big sigh.

4. Imagine your breath is a color. What color is it? There's no wrong color; just see what color comes to you. You can also assign it a color. Let's say pink is for love, blue is for healing, green is for grounding, yellow is for happiness, purple is for intuitiveness, orange is for forgiveness, and white is all of them combined.

5. Now imagine that color wrapping around you like a protective cocoon. Every time you breathe in, your breath is reformed. Every time you breathe out, you send that energy into the Universe.

6. Focus on a good friend. Send that light to them.

7. Now focus on a difficult person. Send that light to them.

8. Focus on the Universe. Send that light to it. You can actually see it radiating in all directions above you and below you, to the east, west, north, and south of you.

Each time you breathe in, you continue to receive the light. You are not just giving away your light. You are giving *and* receiving. This is the true balance of empathy.

ESSENTIAL OILS FOR AN EMOTIONAL EMPATH

Never use essential oils directly on the skin. Always dilute essential oils with a carrier oil like almond oil, grapeseed oil, coconut oil, or olive oil. Essential oils are incredibly concentrated. A few drops are generally all that is needed. Practice aromatherapy by diffusing essential oils or sprinkling a few drops on a handkerchief or pillow.

- **Geranium:** Geranium essential oil is great to use when you are peopled out and need to rebalance or clear yourself of depressed and anxious thoughts.

CRYSTALS FOR AN EMOTIONAL EMPATH

Empaths are sensitive and very intuitive. Because of this, the empath absorbs both positive and negative energies from other people and their surroundings. Empaths naturally want to take care of people, and they often become drained in body, mind, and soul as a result. Crystals are an amazing tool to help. The best crystals for empaths protect the energy field (sometimes called an aura), shield an empath from negative emotions, and keep the empath grounded. You can wear these crystals as a piece of jewelry, put them in your purse or pocket, or lay them near you.

- **Malachite:** This crystal is a beautiful green color. It has the ability to clear and release stagnant energy. It works with your heart chakra, which is the center where an emotional empath holds the emotional pain of themselves and of others. This crystal is great for kids to keep in their pocket too. It doesn't remove the gift of compassion. Instead, it strengthens it—and with healthy boundaries.

- **Selenite:** Selenite is a high-vibration crystal that offers healing, a sense of inner peace, and clarity. Not only can it help cleanse other crystals (or tarot or oracle cards) of negative energies, is creates a peaceful environment. I keep a piece of selenite under every mattress in my home. And when I travel, I take a piece and put it on the nightstand to cleanse the energy of the hotel or home I'm staying in.

AFFIRMATIONS FOR AN EMOTIONAL EMPATH

- Surround me with love and light.
- Help me flow in the light of positivity and energy.
- Help my attention stay focused toward the good.
- All is well.
- I oversee my emotions.
- I recover quickly from obstacles.
- I make myself a priority.

FOUR
The Intuitive Empath

ARE YOU AN INTUITIVE EMPATH?

1. Does your intuition give you a clear picture of something beyond the surface level?

2. Are you able to help others verbalize what they are feeling?

3. Are you a natural go-to for advice or counseling?

4. Do you suffer from an autoimmune issue or chronic pain?

5. Do you trust your gut when deciding on a matter?

6. Can you sense the emotions of your loved ones even if you aren't physically with them?

7. Do you like to stay busy and focused?

8. Are you quick to spot when someone is lying?

9. Do you consider yourself creative or artistic?

10. Do you need alone time to rebalance yourself, then bounce back and want to be with people, and continue that cycle?

If you answered yes to more than two of these questions, you are likely an intuitive empath. You aren't crazy. You are simply someone with a gift that can be developed and better managed.

If you don't feel like you resonate with this trait, continue to read this chapter because it will help you understand someone in your circle who has this trait.

. . . .

Everyone can tap into their intuition and psychic senses. Some have a natural gift, while others must work at developing it. The more you decide to embrace your true self—even if it comes from opening yourself up to receive good, bad, and sometimes ugly messages—the less complicated your life becomes. Sometimes tapping into your intuition and psychic senses requires you to color outside the lines. Trusting your intuitive nudges can keep you out of harm's way, help you avoid stress, and lead to easier decision-making (even if the decisions might not be ones you want to make).

It makes sense that an empath is intuitive; after all, an empath is highly sensitive. All empaths are intuitive, but not all empaths are intuitive empaths. The thing is that intuitive empaths are skilled observers. They pick up on a person's body language, mood, and energy level. They can decipher things beyond their sight. They "see" with their intuition and gut feelings. They know that synchronicities aren't random; they are messages or intuitive nudges. Many intuitive empaths are naturally psychic.

For a long time, I thought being an empath was a curse. Oh, heck, I thought that yesterday! Of course, there are pros and cons to being any type of empath. I personally don't love change. I don't love coloring outside the lines, yet being an intuitive empath takes me out of my comfort zone and screams for me to do so. The kick is that most times, leaving your comfort zone leads to wonderful things. You discover beautiful new places, meet fantastic people, and make amazing memories.

Avoiding the challenges of being an intuitive empath speaks to a lack of tools. While not every intuitive empath dreads spontaneity, the point is that when gifted with a challenging trait, you must constantly make a conscious choice not to run back to your comfort zone.

LIFE AS AN INTUITIVE EMPATH

An intuitive empath is a finely tuned antenna that picks up everything about everyone. The challenges come when the empath isn't tuned to the proper frequencies, and they exhaust themselves deciphering information that might be more they can handle. They can, though, learn how to better adjust their signals to live a healthier and happier life with their gift.

EMOTIONAL DETECTIVES

Intuitive empaths know what others feel without needing to be told, and they have an unusually sharp sense for whether someone is telling the truth or lying. They can "read" a room by detecting the tiniest changes in facial expressions, shifts in tone of voice, and slight adjustments in body language. The difference between an intuitive empath and someone who is trained to do that is it comes naturally to an intuitive empath; they rarely even realize how in tune they are. This might be because many intuitive empaths grew up in toxic or emotionally heightened environments where picking up on subtle shifts in their environment or the people in it was a matter of survival.

One of my clients, Alexia, was an intuitive empath. She grew up in a household with her mother, father, two brothers, and maternal grandmother. She and her siblings were only a few years apart, so there was always hustle and bustle happening. It was a loving household, she explained to me, until her father died of cancer.

"Nobody even told us he had cancer, but I knew something was wrong. It wasn't even like he had just gotten cancer and died. He apparently had cancer for year. To this day, I don't know if they didn't take it seriously or if his doctors told him to live life to the fullest because there was nothing to do.

"I was a freshman in high school. It was a Friday. We were heading into Christmas break and friends invited me over for a sleepover, and my parents told me to go. Something told me not to. My mom wasn't a crier, and I caught her crying in the bathroom. She said she thought she was getting a cold from Dad. Dad was lying in bed, something he never did, and said he had a bad headache. Something just didn't feel right, but I went to my friend's house."

As she talked, Alexia looked like she was transporting thirty years back in time. Her eyes were distant and her body language was tense.

"My friend's mom woke me up and told me I needed to go home. I was confused. It was the middle of the night, but I knew. I knew Dad was gone. I was only ten minutes away, but I'll never forget the reflection of the ambulance lights on my home. I ran in to see them putting my daddy into a black body bag and zipping it up. Of course, Mom was a mess. My brothers were too, but they both held it together.

"It was my grandma who took control of the household because Mom became unhinged. If I was sassy, whether I really was or whether she just construed my behavior as sassy, she would hit me. I could be putting cereal in my bowl, not saying a word, and *wham!* She would slap me in the face. She never hit me before Dad's passing. I literally became her punching bag.

"I became on edge, trying to sense her mood so I could be prepared. In the movies when something bad is going to happen, you hear the eerie music, right? I tried to train my intuition to hear the music before it came so I could duck or escape. I had to learn her energy to try and avoid my own mother before she swooped in and attacked me. Even at nighttime, I would be sound asleep, and she would bolt through my door and start hitting me. You know, I wanted so badly to put the blankets over my head, but all I could think of was my father's body bag. It was challenging."

The type of trauma Alexia experienced can cause hypervigilance. If an outsider viewed her and her reactions, they might think she was being paranoid, but she could read the situation accurately because she was living it. Thankfully, Alexia's mom got help, and so did Alexia, but her intuition stayed locked in.

LIAR LIAR

Because of the hypervigilance that intuitive empaths have, they are natural lie detectors. At some point, everyone lies. Or fibs. Or tells a fishy story. Whatever you want to call it to make you feel better. Sometimes empaths lie too, although when they do, it eats at them. Nothing irks an intuitive empath more than when someone lies to their face and tries to continue the string of lies when they know the person is being a bold-faced liar. An intuitive empath would much rather be spoken to honestly, even if it stings for a bit, than be lied to.

One of the many jobs I do is helping law enforcement with missing persons and cold cases. One of the detectives that often called me when he was stumped on his cases was named Brett. Over the years we'd built a friendship, but I'd never done a reading for him personally. I was surprised when he texted me late one Friday night and asked if he could pick my intuitive brain.

"But this time it's about me, Kristy. It's not a case," he texted.

I picked up the phone and immediately called him.

"I knew my girlfriend was seeing someone other than me," Brett shared. "I asked her over and over, to the point I seemed absolutely crazed and paranoid. She said I was being 'too intense' and used that as an excuse to break up with me. Sure enough, the day after our official breakup, her status on social media changed to 'in a relationship,' and then it was Instagram official with a picture of the dude I knew she was seeing. I knew it. She even accused me of following her, but I didn't have to. I knew it!"

Brett used his gut feelings to protect and serve in his job, but he wasn't the stalker type. Those who are unaware of the gifts of an empath simply won't understand that your feelings are truly another means of seeing without physically having to see.

YOU KNOW THINGS

Once, when I was at a charity event with my husband, I was approached by another intuitive empath. Chuck had left my side to get us drinks, and soon after, a man came up to me.

"You know things," he simply said to me.

I looked at him to see if he'd been a client of mine before and was just trying to be funny, but I didn't recognize him. I also wasn't at the event in a professional sense, meaning I wasn't there as Psychic Medium Kristy Robinett—I was just Kristy Robinett.

"Excuse me?" I smiled, wondering if I'd heard him correctly.

"Wait, that's not a pick-up line," he laughed. "You have this light, and I can see how you observe the room. That you know things. Is it hard to know so much?"

Chuck came back with the drinks and I introduced him to the man, whose name was Dax. It seemed Dax was an intuitive empath as well, but he was raised to believe being an empath was a weakness. He felt as if he had to disguise it.

"I sometimes tell people what they need to hear and not just want they want to hear," Dax said. "It doesn't always go over very well."

I laughed because I knew exactly what he was talking about. An intuitive empath never wants to hurt anyone's feelings. On the contrary, an empath wants everyone to learn to grow and evolve. But this isn't always well received.

I said, "People also will tell you the most intimate things about their life. And that can be odd, but it's also a gift. Look at you, you just came over and told me you are an empath. I bet you wouldn't have told him," I pointed to a random man.

"Funny you chose him. That's my partner. And nope, I try to keep it disguised because he thinks this is all woo-woo."

"Let me one up your woo-woo and tell you what I do for a living."

After a brief synopsis of "I see dead people," we all had a big laugh.

"But, in all seriousness," I said to him. "One of the dislikes an empath has is a liar. It is like nails on a chalkboard to most. How do you feel lying to your partner that, by the way, I can tell you love very much, and vice versa?"

Dax looked at me hard, then scratched the whiskers on his cheek. "You're right," he whispered. "He keeps saying he feels I'm keeping something from him, or I'm not committing to him. I'm so afraid of losing him that I'm not being my true self. But what if…"

I shook my head and waved his last sentence away. "If it's meant to be, it will be. You can even be less woo-woo and more scientific. The term in lieu of empath or psychic is that you are an HSP, or highly sensitive person. It's not a diagnosis per say, but an explanation."

Dax and I exchanged business cards before we left the charity event. I didn't hear from him until a couple months later. He sent me a picture of two wedding rings and a note that read, "He still loved me."

Highly Sensitive Person (HSP)

Being highly sensitive is often misunderstood. And sometimes, it's misdiagnosed as being a dreamer and/or a crybaby. A highly sensitive person, or HSP, was a term coined by psychologist Elaine Aron in the 1990s. Being an HSP is a personality trait that brings both strengths and challenges. In essence, being an HSP is part of being an empath. But saying you're an HSP sounds fancier, more official, and less woo-woo.

Within the last ten years, the empath trait has become much better known and more understood, even in the scientific community. Characteristics of a highly sensitive person include:

- Deep thinker
- Deep feeler
- Makes deep connections
- Connects the dots quicker than most

- Easily picks up on emotional cues from others
- Focuses on textiles and tastes
- Hears things better than most
- Can be an introvert or an extrovert, and sometimes can flip the switch between both

I Cry a Lot, But I'm Still Cool

I laid on the red couch in my living room, my head on the tan pillows. Tears streamed silently down my face. I was so numb I couldn't feel my arms. I could hear my husband, Chuck, happily singing in the kitchen. I heard him start the dishwasher and come toward the living room, so I quickly wiped my face. I hadn't worn any makeup that day, so I was safe from Alice Cooper eyes or smeared lipstick down my chin. Nonetheless, when you are married to your best friend who intuitively feels your moods without having to say a word, not even a mask can cover up the sad aura.

"Stop it," Chuck gently scolded me. "You are way too sensitive," he said, shaking his head. "You need to be more like me and say &%@* it."

You are way too sensitive. Those words were like gasoline on an already blazing inferno. Those words were constantly used when I was growing up, in school, in the corporate world, with boyfriends, and with an ex-husband. I had decided long ago that being too sensitive was exactly who I was, not a disease or a negative fault.

"He called me fat, Chuck. And then called me a liar. You were there. You heard him. And now you are going to call me too sensitive?" I began crying again, wiping the tears with my hand.

That morning I had gone to Urgent Care to see a doctor because I couldn't lift my knee after another busy paranormal weekend. The doctor's diagnosis was that I was just fat. No, really. His exact words were that because I was fat (not "heavy" or even "extra fluffy"), the extra weight had hurt my knee. The doctor didn't even look at my knee. No X-ray. No exam. Just a "You're fat."

Even if I wasn't "too sensitive," I would think I had a hall pass for being sensitive to that experience. But no matter, I was devastated, and everything after that put me in a funk. I texted my girlfriends, who didn't seem to offer much sympathy. When I whined to friends and received loving support, it still did no good because my pride was bruised, and my sensitivity bone was spinning like the Price is Right wheel. I was too *everything*. I was too numb, too mad, too sad, and everything in between. And probably too sensitive too, but it was who I am. It *is* who I am.

Chuck realized what he said was not at all sympathetic, and he did feel bad. In the meantime, I inundated myself with sappy movies and videos that made me cry and get it out. As I moped, my three-legged orange kitty Archie (Captain Samuel Archibald Robinett of the Seven Seas) climbed up in my lap. He sat there looking up at me with his golden eyes and just wiggled his tail. It was then that I got it. I needed to stop barking (or meowing) and embrace all of me.

If someone calls you too sensitive, say thank you. Because like your eye color, it is just another quality that you have. Now, when someone says I'm too sensitive, I thank them and add, "I know I cry a lot, but I'm still pretty cool." It always makes them laugh.

You don't have to change who you are. In fact, don't ever change. Just learn how to deal with things the best way you can.

When Your Super Sensitivity Is Extra...

- Write or journal.

- Don't avoid your emotions. Be careful not to go to that passive-aggressive place.

- Reach out to your friends. Look around to see who gets you. Remove those who belittle or bully you.

- Feel it. Cry if you want. Scream if you must.

- Sleep. The bedroom is an oasis for sensitive people. Decorate it in soft colors, and remove all clutter if you can.

- Take breaks or mini-vacations.

- Exercise. Yoga, Pilates, and dance seem to work best for sensitive people.

- Shop, but within your means.

- Embrace all of your senses.

- If you can, get a massage. It will reinvigorate you.

- Use crystals to absorb the excess energy.

- Take a bath or shower. Water washes away the excess energy.

Stressors of an Intuitive Empath

Intuitive empaths just know things. They have this uncanny ability to pick up on the emotions of others. When the energy in a room is high and vibrant, empaths feel it. When the room is filled with energy vampires or negative energy, empaths feel like electric eels are shocking their environment. They might feel their own lifeblood being drained. Or the negative energy can feel subtle, like an undercurrent of sorts, that is hard to explain beyond "I just have a feeling." This sometimes makes an intuitive empath seem high-maintenance or intense. It's never intentional, but an intuitive empath has their own set of dislikes that pull them off-course, such as:

- **Advice:** Empaths are asked for advice frequently. They listen to every word and, using their sense of knowing, carefully give advice. It might not be what the person wants to hear, but it's good advice. An empath gets frustrated when they gift time and energy trying to help someone who and then that person doesn't follow through with the advice.

- **Being Rushed:** An intuitive empath does better when they are given time to juggle their schedule. As much as they do love to be kept busy, they like to be busy *and* focused. Feeling rushed, especially by an outside party, brings an overwhelming stress that could trickle into a physical issue.

- **Clutter:** Clutter can be a mental weight for an empath. The simpler, more organized, and more accessible an area is, the easier an empath can move through their environment.

- **Conflict:** An intuitive empath prefers the world around them to be peaceful, because when things get heated and conflict brews, they often do one of two things. Either they lash out and run, or they bottle their emotions up and eventually everything comes out. Because of this, empaths are often seen as passive-aggressive people.

- **Crowds:** An intuitive empath tends to stay away from crowds because there are a lot of people that they are "reading" and absorbing energy from.

- **Dump Zones:** An intuitive empath can psychically tune in to the emotional experience of a person, place, or animal. Because of this, the empath is often a comfortable "dump zone," even for complete strangers.

- **Expectations:** An intuitive empath hates to let anyone down, and because of that they will go above and beyond to try and make everyone happy. They feel absolutely crushed if they let someone down, whether it be a loved one, a coworker, or a complete stranger. They aim to be an expert at everything.

- **Faking It:** As much as an intuitive empath strongly dislikes fake people and liars, they often feel they have to put on an act and hide their strengths and pitfalls. It is often exhausting for them to play a certain actor on a certain day with a certain person.

- **Food:** Empaths love good food, but some are picky when it comes to textures of food. They can be easily anxious, sensitive, and/or irritable if given too much caffeine or sugar.

- **Gifts:** It's not that an intuitive empath doesn't like gifts, it's just that they get anxious that they will have to fake their reaction. If they wear a large T-shirt and are gifted a medium, they will try to make it work rather than ask for a gift receipt or confess they are a size large.

- **Personal Failures:** Intuitive empaths are their own worst enemies most of the time. They stew in self-doubt and the would have, could have, and should have's of a situation. They tend to be perfectionists because then, they do not receive critiques that will eat away at their confidence and make them ruminate more.

- **Restrictive Clothing or Jewelry:** Some empaths find certain clothing textures or jewelry too restrictive. An item might be too uncomfortable, itchy, or heavy, or it just "doesn't feel right." Don't fight this instinct; embrace your own style.

- **Sounds:** Empaths are often overwhelmed in places where there is loud, chaotic noise.

- **Smells:** Empaths have an acute sense of smell and can be irritated by certain odors.

- **Visuals:** Empaths have a highly active imagination. So empaths can feel anxious or even physically ill if they view scenes of violence (physical or emotional) or emotional abuse. This can apply to movies, television shows, news stories, or when out and about.

LIGHTS, CROWDS...RUN

Crowds can intensify things for the already over-sensitized empath. In a crowd, it becomes difficult for an intuitive empath to decipher whose energy belongs to who. It can be draining and manifest mental burnout. It is harder to stay vigilant of your boundaries in a crowd, and the energy feels like trying to herd a group of cats for a picture. Many empaths want to run and hide in crowds.

There's a particular store I shop at where every time I visit, I become panicky and feel the fight-or-flight response. Some days are better than others, but there have been instances where I immediately become like a toddler who's lost her parent in the clothes racks. I have even burst into tears in the vacuum aisle because I lost my family somewhere in the store, and of course they never answer their cell phones. An empath's intuitive radar shuts down when panic mode take control.

I brought this up to a friend of mine who works in healthcare.

"Just as some people are sensitive to scent, some are sensitive to noise. The fluorescent lights have a hum and some sensitives—" she gave me a hard glance, "—hear the consistent tone. It can be like nails on a chalkboard to some, agitating. Add in the crowds and the noise of phones going off, chatter, the cash registers, the smells of different things, and it makes perfect sense to me," she validated.

Elaine Aron writes, "Most people ignore sirens, glaring lights, strange odors, clutter, and chaos. HSPs are disturbed by them … Most people walk into a room and perhaps notice the furniture, the people—that's about it. HSPs can be instantly aware, whether they wish to be or not, of the mood, the friendships and enmities, the freshness or staleness of the air, the personality of the one who arranged the flowers."[3]

Everyday things like shopping can be a lot for an intuitive empath. I've found that having a list before I go into this store helps me stay focused. I get in, and I get out. Having a list leaves me no time for fight-or-flight responses or toddler tantrums in the vacuum aisle.

· · · ·

Like shopping, traveling can provide stimulation overload for an intuitive empath. Most people love to travel, and most of the time I'm one of those people. But then there was my trip to Vegas. Now, I know what you are thinking: *An empath going to Vegas sounds like*

....

3. Aron, *The Highly Sensitive Person.*

a nightmare. The crowds, the noises, the lights, and the energy, oh my. But we weren't headed to Vegas for that type of experience. My husband and I were going to hang out with friends for a couple days and then head to Utah, where I was going to teach psychic classes at a beautiful resort in St. George. I figured whatever residual energy I picked up in Vegas, I could dissolve away at the spa.

Our hotel in Vegas was beautiful. The food was delicious. Our time with friends was amazing. All was well. But on our last night in Vegas, we visited a casino and I felt like I was jumping out of my skin. It was like a panic attack, but there wasn't really a reason. Or was there? I was simply agitated. Chuck and I were bickering for no reason. My friends were bickering for no reason. Suddenly, I had to get out of the casino as if it were on fire, so I excused myself back to the room. I took a long, hot shower to cleanse the energy off, and we ordered pizza in the room until I felt stronger and ready to continue the fun.

There were likely many reasons why the panic set in, and it had nothing to do with me, my husband, or our friends. Empaths are in tune with energy, and sometimes we run into it like a brick wall. Let's say a couple had a heated argument in their hotel room or in the hallway of the casino. They might walk away, but they leave residual energy from the argument without any obvious physical evidence that it took place. The empath walks by where the argument happened and feels all of it, and then the empath must do the cleanup.

I was experiencing empathy fatigue, where an empath is bombarded by so much energy that they get moody, irritated, tired, grumpy, etc. If the empath is unaware that this type of reaction is a side effect of being an empath, it can start all sorts of problems in relationships. Thankfully, my husband and my friends understood, so my quick escape wasn't rude, it was an emergency and a requirement.

Hygge

Hygge is a Danish word that means "a cozy quality that makes a person feel content and comfortable."[4] It's a defining characteristic of Danish culture.

Have you seen a dog fluffing a dog bed, going around and around in circles before they lay down? That pet was fluffing the bed's energy, clearing the energy so it felt matched to their own. It's like walking into a location and realizing everything just feels right. Or—the opposite—going somewhere and immediately feeling icky in a way that has nothing to do with the physical location. Some people can even feel that energy on paper or have an innate sense of knowing. Most don't even realize it's an empath trait.

An unknowing empath might say "I just don't like Vegas" but have no real reason why; nothing bad happened in Vegas, it just didn't feel good. Or someone might say, "I don't like Florida." Nobody can convince that person that Florida is amazing; it's the way they feel. It works the opposite, too: by being drawn to a certain place, even if you've never visited the place you feel so connected to. That is hygge.

Empaths who work in the real estate industry are often amazingly successful because they can match the energy of a person to the energy of a location.

EMPATHS ARE THE HEALERS OF THE WORLD

Empaths heal others on a soul level. An empath can lock in on a person's feelings, whether that person is feeling happiness, grief, fear, sadness, or pain. More often than not, the empath feels obli-

....

4. *Merriam-Webster*, s.v. "hygge," accessed October 15, 2021, https://www.merriam -webster.com/dictionary/hygge.

gated to step in and flood the person with their healing energy. They want to help heal as many people as they can, but unfortunately this can become an invitation for psychic burnout. An empath doesn't heal for praise; it's a natural calling. It's no wonder many empaths turn to healing fields. If they decide on a non-healing field, they continue to be the go-to for their family, friends, coworkers, and complete strangers.

Being an empath can be challenging, especially when you are a healer. It's a fine line of mastering the emotional energy and honoring your boundaries while leaving yourself open enough to help. Some healers get jaded, feel overwhelmed, and withdraw.

My dad had triple bypass surgery in September 2018, and just two days later he was transferred to the regular cardio floor. I was a bit of a basket case, concerned that he should've stayed in the Intensive Care Unit with more one-on-one care. And then there was Bella, one of the nurses on the cardio floor. She was a petite and spunky woman who had a dragon's glare and a sharp tongue. I questioned everything, trying to be my dad's medical advocate, and although Bella answered my questions, she did so in a semi-combative way.

"I'm not liking his nurse," I told my husband as we both sat in my dad's room.

Chuck just rolled his eyes at me in reply.

"I have a business call, but I'll be back to take care of this," I warned Chuck and my dad, then walked toward a private waiting room down the hall.

While waiting for the call, I allowed myself to take in all the nearby energy. That's when I saw Bella. I watched as she buzzed around the cardiovascular floor preparing orders, answering the patients' persistent calls, and hiding her yawns. Well, she was trying to hide her yawns. She stood against the wall and closed her eyes in what looked like an attempt to ground and reset. When Bella opened her eyes, she noticed I was watching and we both blushed.

"Want to sit with me for a minute?" I asked, pointing at the chair next to me. "We can tell them I asked you to give me an update on my dad."

She shyly nodded and sat down. "I really have no time for rest. I've got this phone and this pager, and then this phone," she pointed at all of the equipment popping out of her pockets.

"You are understaffed and overworked," I commented. "How many hours do you work?"

"Twenty hours, two days a week."

I thought I misunderstood her. "Twenty hours a week?"

"No, twenty hours one day and twenty hours a couple days later," she corrected. "I'd love more hours, but these dark circles would probably get darker, and I want to still be the best nurse I can be."

"Where's home?" I asked her, her accent giving away that she wasn't from Ann Arbor, Michigan.

She smiled. "Brazil. I miss it there, but this is a better life. I just wish I could go home for a visit more often, and I hope my next visit is soon. My mom isn't doing well, and it will probably be the last time I see her."

I looked at Bella, seeing her demeanor soften even more.

"I can tell you are an empath too," Bella sighed. "It's not easy, is it?"

I nodded in agreement. "Hospitals are intense for me, so I give you a lot of credit. Can I share with you something I do when things are heavy?"

Bella glanced down the hallway to see if there were any fires she needed to put out, but all was clear, so she said, "Sure."

"I do something I call 'wiping the crumbs.' I physically wipe away the energy like I've got crumbs on my shirt. I ask my angels to help me wipe the crumbs when I might not recognize I'm in the lion's den of energy." I demonstrated by taking my left hand and doing a wiping motion down my right arm. Then I wiped my right hand down my left arm. Then I wiped down my chest, stomach, and legs with both arms. I finished by shaking it out like I was shaking a tablecloth.

"I like that. I'm absolutely going to try that. Thank you, Kristy." All of her phones and pager lit up at once. "Back to work. And back to your dad, who, by the way, is doing great."

Bella rushed off down the hall just as my cell phone rang.

A couple days later, my dad was released from the hospital. Bella stayed an hour over the end of her shift to help with his release paperwork and walked with us down to the parking lot.

"Now, I don't want to see any of you back on my floor," she growled. She leaned over and gave my dad a gentle hug. "Got it?"

We both nodded, and she turned to me. "Treasure this time," she said, and with a quick hug and a wipe of a few tears, she turned around and quickly walked away.

Healers want to heal. But sometimes, healers build a wall to compartmentalize in order to survive.

HOW HEAVY IS YOUR BACKPACK?

I was walking down Main Street at Disney World in Orlando, Florida, when I saw her. Her brunette hair was in a messy bun. She gracefully handled three small backpacks and a sippy cup while pushing a baby in a stroller while young twin girls held hands and zigzagged in front. Her husband, handsome and very put together, stared forward. He didn't hold a backpack. He didn't push the stroller or hold the girls' hands. He was on a mission, oblivious to the struggles his wife was having. I knew they were together because the family all wore matching shirts, except the mom had a giant grape juice stain on the left side of Mickey's face.

I ended up heading the same direction as the family. By the time we all found our way to the teacups, the baby was sound asleep in the stroller. The parents played rock paper scissors to determine who was going to take the girls on the teacups and who was going to stay on the bench. The mom took a seat on the bench while the girls ran ahead with their father to begin their thirty-minute wait for the ride.

My adult kids had ventured off and my husband was browsing in a shop, so I was simply enjoying myself without having to run to a Fast Pass or lunch reservations. I sat down on the bench next to the woman. I caught her eye and smiled, reminiscing in my mind about when my kids were that age, but refraining from an "I remember those days" spiel that nobody really cares about. Instead, I offered, "You're doing a great job. They will have amazing memories. And I know it's hard, but look at how elegantly you're doing it."

The woman laughed and shook her head with an emphatic no. As if to put an exclamation mark on it, she pointed to Mickey's purple face.

"Mickey needed a drink too. Maybe next time, try something with some alcohol," I said in sympathy. "Hopefully, Epcot is next," I added. Epcot allowed you to order a drink and carry it around the park. It was a parent's happy place.

"Oddly enough, it is," she giggled. "But I won't drink. I'll let Rod, my husband, partake."

It was none of my business why she wouldn't order a drink. She might've been a recovering alcoholic or on medication or breast-feeding. I felt like a fool for even teasing her about it, but she added,

"Rod is the one who needs the break. He's having a hard time handling all the kids and his job and...Well, sometimes, life."

It's not your place, Kristy, I yelled at myself, trying to hush my mouth. I so badly wanted to ask why she didn't deserve a break too. Instead, I clenched my lips together and smiled. Her baby boy stirred, and she fussed with him for a minute until he fell back asleep. Then she took a deep breath and sank back into the bench. "Maybe I need a break too," she confessed.

Forget about staying out of it. People paid me for advice, so I decided to take this as an opportunity to speak up and maybe do her a favor. At least, that's what I tried to convince myself I was doing.

"See all those backpacks you were holding?" I pointed to the ground, where she had dropped them all beside her.

The woman nodded at me, one eyebrow raised in question.

"Remember how heavy they were and how you were struggling, but you kept forging ahead anyhow? You didn't ask your husband for help, ask the girls to take one, or even set them under the stroller."

She nodded again.

"Can I tell you my own backpack story?"

"Sure thing. I need the rest anyhow!" she smiled.

I began, "I lugged a backpack diaper bag around when my kids were little. My daughter was two and a half years older than my son, so when they were little, it was a lot of stuff, as you know. I didn't always empty out the bag like I should've, and one week I noticed that my back was hurting. My husband lifted the backpack and jokingly asked me if I was lugging rocks in the bag, and I laughed in response.

"'Well, I'm not carrying that load,' he told me.

"So, I did. I picked up the bag and couldn't believe how heavy it was, but I continued to ignore it and went on my way. One day, baffled as to why the bag was so heavy, I finally dumped it out. And I found…rocks. Lots of rocks. Apparently, my daughter was finding rocks on the playground and, when I wasn't looking, she was stowing them in a pocket in the backpack, and I was carrying it. It was hurting my back. But I kept doing it until I got so fed up that I stopped, but not before I was tired and hurting.

"We are strong females. We are nurturers. We tell ourselves we need to ignore pain, emotionally and physically, but in the meantime, we get burned out. Yet we keep doing it. Over and over, in an unhealthy cycle. We don't want to admit that we are burned out, because that might make us weak. We see the pain of all those around us, and it's as heavy as rocks, and we put that in our energetic backpack. And we carry that energy. It's your kids, which it honestly should be because they are little. It's your husband. It's friends and parents and coworkers and sometimes even strangers, because you have that backpack wide open for people to throw their rocks in. Your backpack is heavy.

"They say the definition of insanity is doing the same thing over and over and expecting a different result. Those backpacks you are carrying aren't the only thing you are carrying."

I didn't mean to make anyone cry, especially at the most magical place on earth, but there she was, sobbing and staring at me with her mouth agape. I felt awful and went to apologize for opening my mouth, but then her twins came running up out of the crowd, excited that a princess was nearby. The girls wanted to get in line immediately. Before words were exchanged, the family dispersed to continue their busy day. I had to trust that what I said was what needed to be said and that I didn't ruin this woman's trip.

The next day was our Epcot day, or what my husband referred to as "drinking around the world day." My family was all above drinking age, so everyone was extremely excited.

We were passing through Morocco when I heard someone yelling, "Hey! Hey!" My husband pointed to a lady furiously waving our way. It was the brunette woman from the day before, waving and smiling. She raised a frozen daiquiri and pointed to her husband, who was holding one of the backpacks. *It's a start*, I thought. I gave her the thumbs up and matched her huge smile. And I finally breathed a sigh of relief, because I had honestly felt terrible about making her cry.

"What was that all about?" Chuck asked.

I simply said, "I taught her yesterday how to properly hold a backpack that wouldn't hurt her as much."

Chuck shook his head at me in confusion but decided not to ask for clarification.

That's typical empath energy. We are sponges for the energy around us. Emotional energy. Interpersonal energy. Systemic energy. Planetary energy. We get drained *so* easily. It takes a lot to be out in the world, being a sponge for everything, without getting weighed down by it all. It's like being a magnet and walking around when there are little metal chips flying around everywhere—when energy flies by an empath, it sticks. Only energy is invisible. A lot of the time I don't even realize I'm absorbing the energy of a place or channeling the emotions of the people around me, but I am all the time.

The Anxious Empath

Do you know how exhausting it is to drag luggage around an airport? I once checked my luggage with the airline and only had my purse. It was the most freeing experience to walk through an airport without lugging all that weight behind me. I had never done that before because I liked to control where my luggage was. If I had it with me, it was safe and it wouldn't get lost. I wouldn't have to figure out how to find the luggage retrieval area. But was it really me being controlling, or was it my anxiety? Probably both.

An empath often works harder than necessary because they think this will be helpful or create less work for someone else, or whatever other excuse they find. But actually, they are causing more work for themselves. This causes pain and energy drain, and sometimes even arguments. Carry only what you need—and I'm not just talking about luggage.

SUPERNATURAL BLUE LIGHT SPECIAL

One thing that is quite unusual about intuitive empaths is that supernatural phenomena seems to follow them. Many intuitive empaths have had various supernatural experiences, from near death experiences to out-of-body experiences to the paranormal, but this isn't necessarily a prerequisite that determines whether you are an intuitive empath or not.

I'm the person who continually breaks vacuum cleaners, of all things. I pop lightbulbs and streetlights as if I have a superpower. Right now, our camera on our newish car reads fuzzy, and my laptop keeps giving me squiggly lines. The manager at the local phone store knows me by name, and I can't wear a watch without having a ridiculous amount of backup batteries. It's called "slider phenomenon," a term coined by paranormal author Hilary Evans.[5] This electrical phenomenon happens when a person goes through intense

....
5. Evans, *The SLI Effect.*

emotions such as anger, deep sadness, or even overwhelming excitement. An empath tends to be more prone to this gift/curse.

Then there are the paranormal experiences. An empath draws people to their light like a moth to a flame, and they do the same for the other side. Just as an empath is an amazing listener and loving caregiver to the living, those who have passed away see the empath's light and seek it out. Without proper understanding, many empaths are afraid of this, and they try to turn it off. Some succeed.

I'm not sure if you are as old as I am, but back in the day, Kmart was a bustling discount chain store, a lot like a Walmart. Every so often, a clerk would get on the loudspeaker via a corded telephone and announce that there was a blue light special. The clerk would announce the aisle and sometimes what it was. Like, "Hi, Kmart customers. This is Kristy and I'm here by the women's socks. We are having a blue light special. Right now, every pair of socks you buy, you get two free. Come get your socks and your coupon. I'll only be here for five more minutes."

Sounds like I know what I'm talking about, right? I was that Kmart clerk, and I loved announcing blue light specials. In the women's socks aisle, I would stand there with my big blue light flashing, calling out to customers to buy socks even though they didn't really need them. For Kmart it was a marketing ploy, but for me it was a chance to talk to interesting people and to teach myself to handle said interesting people.

Apparently, spirits see empaths as big, blue lights. Just joking, but it is an answer to a question I'm often asked: "How do spirits find people who can help them?" And that blue light special is also felt and/or seen by fellow empaths; empaths recognize their kind. But every empath needs to know they oversee how much energy they receive. An empath can shut off their blue light. An empath can take the phone off the hook. Empaths are allowed to return that energy to sender, whether the energy is alive or the energy has passed on.

There is a stigma that empaths are introverts, but that's not always the case. Most empaths love people—they just don't like being around too many people all the time. The reason why empaths withdraw is because of energy overload, and without the proper tools, they put up a lot of walls to deal with all the emotions they feel. This is simply masquerading instead of correcting the issue.

ROAD CLOSED–ROAD WIDE OPEN

An intuitive empath sometimes gets stuck in the same rut, whether it's ordering the exact same thing every time they go to a restaurant or going home from work the same way every day because they know that way. Intuitive empaths like their typical road, because then they don't have to go a different way. Scary detours and difficult roads can lead us to beautiful places if we stop allowing fear to take over. Nothing changes unless something changes. Instead of driving the familiar route, take a new road. You won't always know where you're headed, but you don't have to have it figured out either. After you take that unfamiliar road, you will have learned something new. You will have grown. Intuitive empaths want to cheer on everyone else's growth, but they are afraid to grow themselves.

Tell that to my husband.

The sign read "road closed ahead," but my husband rarely paid attention to signs.

"They are probably lying, and the road was fixed," he told me.

Now, we've been married long enough for me to know not to bother arguing with him. And sure enough, we were stopped by large construction barrels, along with another six cars who also didn't pay attention to signs, and now we had to turn around. (We've also been married long enough for me to know not to add an "I told you so" to the sideways look I gave him.)

For some odd reason, this road closure left him feeling defeated.

"I don't want to turn around, and I don't want to take the detour," he sighed, still stopped at the closure.

"There's a street that way." I pointed to the right. Let's take that and see where it leads."

"But we don't know where it's going to lead, and the GPS isn't working."

I shrugged. "Try it anyway. If all else fails, we'll end up back here and make another decision."

As you might've guessed, we took the detour, and everything turned out fine. Better than fine! We found ourselves looking at the most beautiful landscape that was just a couple of miles away from our home. We slowed down to yell out "cow" and "horse," as if the grazing animals needed to be reminded what they were; we marveled at the cascading trees that darkened the road, only to open to a beautiful lake with swans happily swimming. And then the road led us right to another street that took us home.

IN A HURRY AND EXHAUSTED

The million-dollar question is whether being an empath is a superpower or a super stressor, a blessing or a curse. It might just be both. Brady, a long-time client of mine, came to see me. He was stressed, but he was upset that he was stressed. He needed some empath coaching.

"I wish I didn't give crap about anything," Brady told me. "Whoever said this was a gift was never an empath. It feels like it's controlling me," he confessed. "I'm spinning trying to help this person and that person. My mom is sick. I'm trying to be with her. My dad is high-maintenance and feeling like he's not getting enough attention, so I'm trying to be with him. My wife is feeling left out and telling me I'm not as active with the kids as I should be, so I'm trying to be with them. And if that wasn't enough, I'm working a job I don't love but I don't hate, but I think my boss thinks I'm phoning it all in. Maybe I am, but something has to give."

"Is it you?" I asked. "Do you think what you are giving is tending to yourself?"

Brady nodded emphatically. "I'm doing all I can, though. I'm trying to make everyone happy and if I have to sacrifice myself, I will do it. I might not have long with my mom or my dad."

"Or they only have time with you if you keep up this schedule. Is it worth that?"

"You can't pour from an empty cup. Yeah, yeah, I've heard it. You've heard it. But sometimes you have to make exceptions."

Oh, I understood where he was coming from. If I had a dollar for every time someone threw the whole "you can't pour from an empty cup" back at me, I'd be a millionaire myself. The truth is, being an empath is a blessing. I know this because I've seen it enrich so many people's lives. Being an empath is a curse. I know this because people take advantage of the best of you. It's a sneaky balance that is hard to maintain when life is constantly throwing curveballs your way, all the time.

Just like female empaths, male empaths feel everything. There is, however, a bit more of a stigma about it for males. If a woman cries, okay. But if a man cries, they are often considered weak. At a young age, many boys are taught that real men don't cry. Guess what? Real men *do* cry, and it doesn't make the man any less of a man. Men get overwhelmed with all their responsibilities just as women do. They also need self-care just as much as women do. Their self-care may look different. While women may go out with the girls and talk about how they are feeling, men rarely do that. Often, they play pool, golf, watch sports, or do another activity to numb the sensitivity.

There is such a thing as an alpha empath. This is a trait that both men and women can have. An alpha empath may not cry or react in public like a typical empath, but in private they do. They are gentle but strong. They tend to be natural leaders. They tend to be voices for the underdogs. Alpha empaths are also not as likely to be manipulated as most empaths are because they are not afraid of calling someone out. Brady reminded me of an alpha empath.

Brady decided to sit down with his family and express his exhaustion. They had no idea. Probably because the more someone throws their hat in the ring, the more things are going to be expected of them. Brady decided he couldn't keep volunteering to do everything. It didn't mean he wasn't capable or that he was weak—it meant he was human. Sometimes empaths forget that asking for help is also a superpower.

I DARE TO DREAM

Dreams are free psychic readings, and intuitive empaths are often dream empaths. They bypass the conscious world to receive intuitive information from the Universe. This type of empath is good at remembering their dreams. The dream empath must take it one step further by learning about the symbolism in their dreams, because a dream empath mines for knowledge, intuition, and inspiration through that subconscious space of sleep.

When someone asks me, "How did you sleep?" most of the time I answer with a deep sigh. I love sleep. I love naps. Mostly because I don't sleep well. I'm often visited by the spirit world at nighttime. Spirits show up in my dreams, and sometimes I even have night-time visits with living people. Or that's what they say.

"Kristy, I had the most amazing dream with you in it. I was feeling lost about a situation and in my dream, you were there, and you gave me advice that makes sense. Now I know what to do!"

I get these emails weekly. I joke that I'm going to start sending invoices to these people. It's not even that I'm astral traveling to people and setting up a booth to give advice. (But that would be cool, right?) The person is simply looking for someone they look up to that will give them advice, and they project that person to be me.

Have you ever had a dream that someone close to you was going to have a baby, and they announced a pregnancy soon after? Or have you ever had a dream of a loved one who passed away that felt real? A dream can convey feelings, thoughts, ideas, desires, and other psychological factors that may lie buried when you're awake. Dreams are also said to convey information from outside of your-self, such as: spiritual guidance, premonitions, and interactions with loved ones who have passed on.

Getting lost in your mind—whether from sleeping, meditating, or daydreaming—can be filled with healing and intuitive informa-tion. Keep in mind that dreams speak in symbols and talk in a rep-resentative language just like poetry, so they are rarely literal.

For a dream empath, naps are a healthy elixir. An empath is so busy picking up other people's energy (along with picking up the energy of everything else) that it can cause overstimulation. And overstimulation can cause mental and physical exhaustion, so a nap is a positive way to recharge and regroup for many empaths.

Dream Shielding

Dreams can be overwhelming for an intuitive empath. Too much of anything is too much, and that includes dreams. Sleep should be serene and healing so you can get a good night's sleep. But the astral plane is filled with an array of doors that lead to the good, the okay, and the evil. Without proper shielding, you could accidently open the wrong door. So how does an empath shield themselves to make sure that doesn't happen?

- **Crystals:** Keeping crystals such as kyanite, moonstone, or calcite by your bedside can calm the spirit.

- **Prayer:** Expressing your worries and needs to the Universe before falling asleep helps to surrender them and allows someone/something else to take the wheel.

- **Affirmations:** An affirmation such as "I am protected" can be helpful before bedtime.

- **Meditation:** Visualize a shield of protection around you. It can be a bright light of protection, a stone wall, a wall of flames, a moat, a spirit guide, or whatever you want it to be. The barrier you choose keeps unwanted energy away from you and locks the negative doors so you couldn't open them even if you tried.

TOOLS FOR AN INTUITIVE EMPATH

There are many steps that an intuitive empath can take to be as healthy and happy as possible. I've included some suggestions for essential oils, crystals, and affirmations, as well as tips and a meditation for intuitive empaths.

THE POWER OF BECAUSE

One of the greatest gifts that an intuitive empath has is the ability to read other people through slight energy shifts. These shifts don't always make sense to an empath and can be especially confusing for those around an intuitive empath.

My mom and dad used to tell me "because" wasn't an explanation for anything: "Why did you do that?" "Because." "Why are you crying." "Because." But here's the thing: For an intuitive empath, "because" is a complete sentence. No other explanation is needed. Because it's not always understood at the time. I just had a feeling. I felt a vibe. Because. It sums up an intuitive empath completely.

MEDITATION EXERCISE FOR AN INTUITIVE EMPATH

This meditation is similar to the advice I gave to the lady at Disney. I do this exercise every single night.

• • • •

Get comfortable, close your eyes, and call upon any archangels, angels, ascended masters, etc., to put a white light of protection around you.

Then envision a doorway. You are at peace and feel secure, so you walk through it. As you look up, you find that you are on a beautiful pathway that is filled with so much to explore. Bunnies are hopping and birds are singing the sweetest song. The sky is the most beautiful color of blue, and the grass is greener than you've ever seen. The air is filled with the most amazing scents from the flowers that grow all around you.

As you take a step forward, you feel your body is heavy. It's stopping you from adventuring. You notice there's a backpack on your back that feels like it might be holding boulders.

This backpack is full of your worries, troubles, concerns, and negative feelings. You've been carrying them for a long time. It wasn't until you noticed the backpack that you noticed your shoulders and back ache. Your neck feels stiff, and even your feet are crying at the weight. You try to remove the backpack, but it just won't come off.

A being of light appears on your pathway. It might come in the form of a human, an animal, a shadow, a feeling, a voice, or whatever is comfortable for you. This being of light points to an amazing bridge that overlooks a roaring waterfall. It's weird that you never even saw it there; you were too consumed with the burden of the backpack.

It's hard, but you make it to the bridge, and slowly you are able to shrug off the backpack. You open it up and inside are rocks. Some are tiny; some are large. They each have a name of a concern, a worry, or a negative feeling on them.

The being of light tells you to dump them. You might take handfuls and dump them over the side of the bridge and into the rushing water. Or you might take them one by one, reading what is written on the stone before throwing it over.

With each stone dumped, you feel more and more relaxed and free. When you are done, check to see if there are any rocks hiding at the bottom of the bag. You might want to put your backpack back on, or you might throw the backpack over the side of the bridge.

You feel lighter and happier already. Now you are free to adventure and explore.

When you are ready, go back to your doorway and walk through it back into the now. Understand that anytime you want discard excess energy or heavy energy, you can return to this place.

PROTECTION EXERCISE FOR AN INTUITIVE EMPATH

Before you take your daily bath or shower, set your intention. It might be for spiritual protection, love, money, or to remove negative energy from your life. You can say it in your head or out loud. Say something like, "I set the intention of (choose your intention) and ask my angels and guides to help me with this."

As you stand under the shower water or get into the bath, envision the water washing all the negative energy away, cleansing all that is weighing you down in body, mind, and spirit. The water replaces the negative energy with a bubble of protection, and anything that doesn't serve your intention will bounce off of it.

As you dry off, be sure to thank your guides and angels, knowing that you are loved.

ESSENTIAL OILS FOR AN INTUITIVE EMPATH

Never use essential oils directly on the skin. Always dilute essential oils with a carrier oil like almond oil, grapeseed oil, coconut oil, or olive oil. Essential oils are incredibly concentrated. A few drops are generally all that is needed. Practice aromatherapy by diffusing essential oils or sprinkling a few drops on a handkerchief or pillow.

- **Frankincense:** This oil helps clear the mind of cluttering thoughts so you can feel in tune and intuitive again.

CRYSTALS FOR AN INTUITIVE EMPATH

Empaths are sensitive and very intuitive. Because of this, the empath absorbs both positive and negative energies from other people and their surroundings. Empaths naturally want to take care of people, and they often become drained in body, mind, and soul as a result. Crystals are an amazing tool to help. The best crystals for empaths protect the energy field (sometimes called an aura), shield an empath from negative emotions, and keep the empath grounded. You can wear these crystals as a piece of jewelry, put them in your purse or pocket, or lay them near you.

- **Lapis Lazuli:** This is a stone of protection against anxiety and psychic attack. It helps with emotional healing by helping the empath generate clear and concise goals with determination.

- **Chrysoprase and Smoky Quartz:** These are some of the best crystals to deal with recurrent nightmares. Both crystals help bring a feeling of security. They have a gentle, protective energy that counterbalances any negative energy so that the empath can have a peaceful sleep.

- **Amethyst, Moldavite, and Moonstone:** These are great stones if you are looking at increasing your dream powers, especially if you desire lucid dreams. Each one of these crystals protects you from negativity and powerfully helps you receive insight through your dreams. Just as a note, these crystals will not help promote a calm and sound sleep.

AFFIRMATIONS FOR AN INTUITIVE EMPATH

- I am connected to my own inner vision. It is strong, it is clear, and it can be trusted.

- My intuition always knows the best way.

- I'm able to quiet my mind in order to listen to my intuition.

- I release the day and only hold on to good thoughts.

- My dreams are happy and harmonious.

FIVE
The Earth Empath

ARE YOU AN EARTH EMPATH?

1. Do you feel a connection to animals?

2. Do you have a green thumb?

3. Does putting your hands in the dirt make you feel more at peace?

4. Do you sense when there is a full or new moon?

5. Do you feel a sense of peace when you are in nature?

6. Do you experience physical ailments before storms or natural disasters?

7. Have you been called a hippie, or do you consider yourself a hippie?

8. Do bodies of water soothe your soul?

9. Do you love to stargaze?

10. Are you a vegan or vegetarian, or would you like to be?

Since the earth empath has many different categories, you might answer yes to just one of these questions and still be considered an earth empath. You aren't crazy. You are simply someone with a gift that can be developed and better managed.

If you don't feel like you resonate with this trait, continue to read this chapter because it will help you understand someone in your circle who has this trait.

• • • •

An earth empath has several categories. You might be an earth empath, animal empath, plant empath, geosentient empath, or weather empath. An earth empath has a sixth sense regarding anything to do with Universe. Earth empaths are tuned in to nature in some fashion. Plants make them happy and grounded; animals make them feel alive. They might even feel the weather pattern shifts. When the earth is happy, the empath feels happy. When the earth suffers, the empath feels the suffering. Many earth empaths are called hippies, moon maniacs, or tree huggers. The bodies, minds, and spirits of earth empaths are extraordinarily connected with the Universe.

Earth empaths often love activities like hiking, running, biking, rock climbing, photography, and pet rescue. An earth empath also thrives around natural energy sources. They feel energized when they witness a sunrise or sunset, feel the ebb and flow of the lunar phases, and can feel earthly destruction in the core of their being, whether it be a forest fire, earthquake, or air pollution.

LIFE AS AN EARTH EMPATH

Earth empaths need reminders to ground themselves with the earth, often called *earthing*, in order to find inner balance and to keep their aura strong and healthy. Some earth empaths may not even be aware that their desire to run barefoot in the grass, climb a tree, or take long walks on the beach is not just beneficial for their health, it's a requirement to support their life purpose.

THE WHISPERS OF THE TREE

It was a warm Indian summer afternoon. I was about eight years old. My mom and dad had taken me to my favorite place, the local park, to feed the ducks. The hazy sun played peek-a-boo around a large willow tree.

"Never plant a willow tree, Kristy," my mom told me. "They don't have deep roots, so one big storm, *whoosh*." She made a large sweeping motion with her arms. "Gone. And gone with it, any structure near it. They are destructive."

"But they look so magical," I argued.

Of course I argued with my mom. We had constant banter. She tended to be negative, and I always tried to see the positive—and to help her see the positive as well. Round and round we'd go.

I continued to gawk at the curtains of willow branches. They looked like fingers gliding along the top of the small river. Swans danced in and out of the shadows. The tree was so elegant and mysterious.

"And buggy." My mom continued her debate, interrupting my fairy-tale thoughts. "Hear that?"

As if my mom were the cicada charmer, the chorus of what sounded like hundreds, if not thousands, of bugs began to rattle in unison.

"Willows are dangerous," my mom emphasized. Taking my hand, we continued our walk.

Years later, when I was pregnant with my daughter, I was jotting down possible names, as moms-to-be often do: Samantha. Scarlet. Autumn. Ronni. Willow. I made the mistake of sharing my name ideas with my mom.

"Willow?" she huffed. "What kind of name is Willow?"

Mom was never one to keep her opinion to herself.

"Those drooping branches represent tears of sadness. The roots are short, unlike an oak tree. An oak tree has deep roots. But don't call her Oak either," my mom laughed nervously, thinking I might actually take it as a name suggestion.

"In China, willows represent rebirth," I retorted. I had had a miscarriage right before this pregnancy, and after that I was told I'd likely never get pregnant again. This baby was a miracle—what we refer to as a "rainbow baby" in this era—making the name Willow appropriate. "And although they have a different root system than an oak tree, willows actively seek out water and survival any way they can," I added, proud of myself for remembering what I'd learned in botany class. (Who said my college botany class would be useless?)

"Kristy," Mom sighed, irritated with my argument. Knowing I'd likely try to have the last word, she let it go.

I ended up naming my baby girl Micaela, not Willow (although I still love the name). But that wasn't the end of my relationship with the beautiful willow tree.

Recently, I was feeling off-center. I could feel a breakdown coming. And by breakdown, I mean "lying on the shower floor in a tangle of tears." If you've ever been in breakdown mode, there's no ability to reach out. There are no words to speak (even when you get paid to pretend to be a wordsmith). There's ego. There's pride. There's emptiness. There's a blur of emotions that are like tangled Christmas lights; some people are patient at untangling them, and others throw them away in a fit. There's awareness that no matter what you say or do, it won't take the pain away, delete the past, or change the now.

The problem with breakdowns is that you are broken and not thinking. You don't see any way around the pieces, nor can you see that someone else might have the fix-it combination. You are afraid that if you move, you might break more, or you might get cut by the pieces around you. You feel totally stuck. That day, I yelled at my phone screen, begging for someone—anyone—to come up with words I felt I needed. I shouted, "Instead of saying 'I'm here for you' or 'How can I help?', just *help*. Just *do*. Don't wait for the broken to drink a cup of common sense!"

I ended up falling asleep with a hangover-like headache. That headache didn't involve any alcohol—only a lot of residual emotion I had to purge. I awoke to my husband sound asleep next to me with one of our cats snuggled on top of him. Then lightning struck and the wind howled, trying to sweep up my emotions, with thunder following. My clock read 1:35 in the morning. I gazed out of my bedroom window. In the distance, I saw my neighbor's willow tree. My neighbor has a willow tree that sits upon the lake that he affectionately calls his swamp. The tree's branches bent in a frenzy, staying flexible to the uproar and dancing along with the music of the storm.

"See, Mom," I whispered to the heavens, "The willow survived. Maybe the thunder, lightning, and wind aren't the enemy, but the reminder of its strength."

Sometimes we allow the depression of our past and present to shield our view of the beauty around us. Depression dulls the senses like faded curtains. But we can choose to see sadness or new beginnings. We can see a fight or peace. We can see sickness or healing. We have the ultimate choice of which perspective we want to focus on. And breakdowns aren't always bad—they often result in breakthroughs.

Now when I feel ungrounded, I seek out my neighbor's willow tree. I sit by it and talk to it. I let it help me with spiritual growth.

Symptoms of Being Ungrounded

When an earth empath is ungrounded, it can cause all sorts of issues. Before I go into the list of possible issues, I want to remind you that if you are experiencing any of these symptoms, you should visit your doctor or another healthcare professional, as some of these symptoms can be caused by a medical condition.

Ungrounded earth empaths may experience:

- Anxiety with no cause
- Sudden dizziness
- Falling asleep while meditating
- Poor sleep or inability to sleep
- Heaviness in the body
- Feeling spacey
- Feeing emotional
- Craving sugar
- Wanting to eat just junk food
- Nausea

- Mental confusion
- Inability to focus on simple tasks

Ways to Practice Grounding
- Lie flat on the ground and soak up its positivity and strength.
- Be by the water, whether it is a lake, river, or ocean.
- Go moon- or stargazing.
- Smudge yourself with white sage, sandalwood, or cedar.
- Hug a tree.
- Plant some flowers.
- Play with stones or crystals.
- Eat a salad.
- Drink some water.
- Walk barefoot on the grass.

DIRECTIONALLY UNCHALLENGED

One of the most unusual gifts an earth empath has is the ability to feel a location's energy. Many earth empaths are also able to sense their way around a place they've never been before.

Have you ever been out of town and noticed that an area just feels familiar and good? Or been to a location that just feels wrong? If you're an earth empath visiting a new place, you don't have a reason for a place to feel good or bad—it just does. And if you visit a new location and immediately know your way around the area, there is no way to explain how you know that—you just do. Some people believe this inner knowing is connected to a past life, while others believe it's simply matched energy.

Back in the 1970s, there was a children's clothing line that featured mix-and-match separates, but they were matched by the animals on the tags. Bears went with bears, giraffes with giraffes, and so on. The idea behind this was to teach children patterns, colors, and textiles. Well, maybe it was to teach parents too. This combination of your energy and a new location's energy is much like that; if you are wearing the energy of flamingos at a location where everyone is wearing snails, it's a mismatch. But if you show up at a location wearing the energy of tigers and everyone else around you has the energy of tigers, it's a perfect match. When you are in that sweet spot of energy, it's an amazing feeling.

A few years ago, I was filming a television show for a Japanese production company. The show was going to air in Japan and was going to be dubbed in Japanese as well. The crew was from Japan, so the production company arranged for a translator. I was confused about how everything was going to work, but I agreed to a two-day filming schedule.

The team of six met me at my office and I immediately felt comfortable. I was also honored to be chosen to tell my story. Then, on the first day of filming, I was given a gift, and again I felt honored. The filming wasn't difficult either because in an odd turn of events, I found I could understand Japanese! I couldn't speak it, but I understood all the directions and sentiments. I'd never studied Japanese, so I didn't have any idea why or how I was able to understand. But everyone thought it was incredible, and it made the translator's job easier. *You need me to move behind the wall, gesture, and tell the story of that one day while walking toward the other wall? Sure.* I would nod and do what they told me to do in Japanese, and it was exactly what they needed.

When we finished the project, the crew gave me another gift: a picture we took together on the first day. The head of the production team offered me a goodbye hug and gave me a card that had these words of wisdom written in Japanese: *We don't need words to understand. We don't need words to love. Keep being you.*

Whether you call it intuition or simply a spiritual connection, the team and I found our sweet spot of understanding. That experience is the perfect example of an earth empath sweet spot.

LIFE AS A PLANT EMPATH

If you have a natural green thumb, you might be a plant empath. This type of empath is very in tune with plants, trees, and flowers and can form an intuitive connection with them.

PLANTING SEEDS

Plant empaths are connected to the earth in an amazing way. They have faith when a seed is planted in the ground and give thanks. They water the earth with the blind hope that they will receive crops, herbs, and blooms. When Mother Earth lets a plant empath down, they continue to believe that next time, everything will work out.

Once, while giving my garden a drink and swatting away the mosquitos, I felt this overwhelming sense of earth energy around me.

Look around, I heard. *Look at the garden you planted several months ago, believing that come summertime you'd have tomatoes, cucumbers, and peppers. And the perennials that looked pitiful on the clearance rack a few years back, look at how they've filled in nicely. And look at that magnolia tree you planted the year you moved in. You believed that one day you'd find shade under that tree, even though it was just a stick when you planted it. Not once did you think you , doing it all for nothing. Not once did you doubt that you would see your hard work through in your corner of the world. You did all this believing in your tomorrow.*

The "seeing is believing" types won't understand, but plant empaths do. They don't worry that the tree will be toppled by humans or Mother Nature; they believe the tree will grow and be climbed by children, act as shade during a graduation, or be a burial site for their favorite dog.

WEATHERING THE STORM

At some point in our lives, we all go into emotional overload. It's understandable; there's a lot of stress in the world. The news drones on with bleak updates. We aren't interacting with the world the way we used to. Many people have adrenal fatigue, low Vitamin D levels, or poor sleep schedules. There is a heavy load of trauma that people are being inundated with, day in and day out.

We are all weathering a storm right now, but everyone's storm looks different. We aren't all facing the same obstacles, so we can't judge another for what they are discovering in their corner of their world. Some people are battling financial issues, others are navigating divorces, and others are experiencing deep grief from the loss of a loved one. Although we might not understand what another's storm looks like, we can hold everyone in love. We can be more patient. We can be more patient with ourselves. We can pray for others. We can help remind others (and ourselves) that worry robs us of the present moment.

I hope you know that even though you might feel alone, you aren't. You might not see the sunrise or the sunset, but it's there. You might not be able to picture your magnolia tree bringing you shade, but then one day you'll blink and it will be in full bloom.

HUG ON A PLATE

Many plant and/or earth empaths choose to be vegan or vegetarian. It just hurts them too much to eat an animal, or they don't feel well after taking in the energy of the animal that was killed to feed them.

One of my best friends in high school was the first vegetarian I'd ever been around. If I ate a hamburger, she would moo. If I ate anything with ham or bacon, she'd make pig noises. I wanted so badly to be a vegetarian, but I didn't love many vegetables. (Still don't.) "Could I be a chocolatarian?" I'd joke with her.

Those feeling ungrounded may make poor food choices. One of the best ways to become grounded when stressed from the heaviness of the world is to eat yummy food from the earth, as it is truly a hug on a plate.

LIFE AS AN ANIMAL EMPATH

Animal empaths are the people feeding the squirrels and keeping bird feeders filled. They would rather be playing with the neighbor's dog than talking to their neighbor.

The typical animal empath communicates with animals through intuition, intuitively sensing the needs and emotions of animals. Just as an animal empath wants to heal animals, animals love to heal animal empaths.

ANIMAL MAGNET

An animal empath has an exceptional ability to recognize and understand the emotions of an animal. They can interact with the animal and understand their behaviors. Animals are drawn to an animal empath just as much as an animal empath is drawn to animals. Animals have unlimited amounts of love, and they are devoted to those who love them unconditionally. Most animal empaths would rather pet a cat, play with a dog, or brush a horse than deal with people or real-life issues.

I once traveled to a resort in Mexico. Unbeknownst to me, many resorts either have a problem with feral cats or use feral cats to help with rodent issues. One morning at 4:00 a.m., I heard a meow at my hotel door. I thought I was dreaming at first, but the meows got louder to the point that I couldn't ignore them.

I carefully opened my hotel door to find a small white kitten sitting there, as if she were expecting me. "Don't feed it," a friend I had traveled with warned. I didn't. But I did bend down and pet the kitten's head, giving it some love.

The next morning, at 3:00 a.m., I again woke up to meows. This time the cats had multiplied—there were four of them. And they were all sitting there looking at me, as if expecting something. I bent down and simply pet all four cats.

Later that day, I went to the front desk to see if they were aware of the cats and to ask if perhaps someone staying in our room previously had fed them. The hotel staff explained they were feral cats, apologized, and moved our room.

It didn't matter. Early in the morning, again and again, there were the cats, sitting at my door. This continued until I left. Besides the inconvenience of waking up early in the morning, it wasn't too bad—the cats were happy with some pets and then would just run off. The irony was that my friend was allergic to cats, so she wasn't too happy about our nighttime visitors.

I ended up marrying another animal magnet. Chuck and I joke if a neighbor is missing an animal, it will turn up on our front porch. We've had everything from opossums that drink Vernors to a neighbor's rescued raccoons, ducks, chickens, cats, dogs, and more. One day I was working in my office doing a phone session. I looked to my right and was surprised to see a horse looking back at me, standing in front of my window and munching on a bush. I had to tell my client I needed to call them back, explaining I had to call the police because there was a peeping horse. I'm not sure they believed me. The police came right away (small town) and sure enough, the horse down the street had gotten out of its yard. Of course, it found me, just like the feral cats.

· · · ·

Carli was a friend of mine from childhood. Ever since Carli was a young child, she was drawn to animals, and they to her. Almost every picture of Carli included some kind of animal or insect. It was no surprise that she wanted to go into veterinarian medicine, but college is expensive, so she joined the United States Army to help with the cost. Carli did so well that she received a full scholarship, but it came with a deployment to the Middle East. Before her deployment, she took care of soldier's pets. While deployed, she was taking care of horses and other farm animals. Although Carli loved all creatures, she wasn't so fond of spiders. Unfortunately, there's a limitless amount of those in the Middle East, especially camel spiders. They don't have a venomous bite, but they do have a painful bite. They are large and ugly; they look a bit more like a scorpion than a spider. And camel spiders seemed to be drawn to Carli, so much so that it was a joke with her peers.

"They must know I won't hurt them," Carli shuddered. "And if I won't hurt them, they won't hurt me. Hopefully."

One night Carli heard her partner, Elleanor, scream. She ran for their tent, and there was Elleanor, lying on a cot in her sleeping bag. Lying on top of her was a camel spider, inching closer and closer to her face. Carli looked around to see what she could grab it with, but there was nothing. Instead, she started talking to it.

"You don't want to harm anyone. Nobody here wants to harm you. Just go. Just shoo," she said, as if she were talking to a dog or a cat.

The odd thing was, the spider stopped moving up toward Elleanor. It backed up and scooted away.

They both felt relieved and called for another friend to help them de-spider the tent, sweeping them as far away as possible. After the chat, neither Carli nor Elleanor had another camel spider incident that quite as scary.

"There was a pig that showed up at the tent, and that got a bit scary," Carli laughed when she was telling me the story. "It seems I am an animal magnet no matter where I go."

LIFE AS A WEATHER EMPATH

A weather empath can intuitively feel the pressure drop, and many know when a storm is on the horizon. Some weather empaths feel it in their bones, some feel extra tired, and others might get migraines. Some weather empaths feel anxious, get headaches, experience mood swings, and so on. While every weather empath will feel things differently, many are also able to sense natural disasters. They might feel anxious, jittery, or extra sleepy. Also, many weather empaths also sense the lunar phase without looking at a calendar.

It isn't uncommon for a weather empath to have a *knowing* of a natural disaster. On March 10, 2011, my daughter Micaela couldn't get out of bed. Her body was aching, and she was extra sensitive, with tears flowing easily. She never wanted to miss school, but she asked me to call her in sick. She didn't know what was wrong, but she felt that something was wrong—or was about to go wrong. On March 11, 2011, a 9.0 earthquake shook Japan, stirring a deadly tsunami that devastated. It was then that we realized my daughter inherited the empath trait, her own unique empath trait.

A FUNNEL OF EMOTION

One Sunday night, my son came home from his friend's house all excited. His friend's family was going camping Monday through Wednesday, and they had invited him. I rarely told him no. Until then. It wasn't far from home, but something felt wrong in my bones. Literally. My knees hurt and I couldn't seem to catch my breath. My whole being felt off as soon as he asked permission.

"I'm sorry, Connor, I have a weird feeling. I'm gonna have to say not this time."

"But we aren't even doing anything," he whined back at me.

To say he was unhappy with me was an understatement. Monday morning came and I could hardly focus. *Maybe I am coming down with something*, I thought. Until that evening, when a tornado touched down at the campground his friend and parents were staying at. The ninety-five-mile-an-hour winds overturned trailers and tore up tents. It killed one person and injured many.[6] His friend and his family were safe, thankfully.

I obviously wanted to tell my son "I told you so," but instead I told him my gift wasn't trying to hurt him, but keep him safe.

Weather empaths often have intense physical feelings before natural disasters. Some say they feel off or describe a sort of vertigo. These sensations could be connected to solar flares, volcanic eruptions, tornadoes, or hurricanes. And the weather empath doesn't

....

6. "Fierce Storm Slams Michigan Campground, Kills 1."

have to be anywhere near the vicinity of the disaster; they can feel it in New York even if it is happening in Australia.

TOOLS FOR AN EARTH EMPATH

There are many steps that an earth empath can take to be as healthy and happy as possible. I've included some suggestions for essential oils, crystals, and affirmations, as well as tips and a meditation for earth empaths.

COMMUNICATE WITH THE EARTH

To communicate intentionally with Earth, you can ask "How do you feel?" and then listen to its response. Be open to all of your intuition's nudges. The earth is your oracle; it offers healing teachings.

Mother Nature rules all, but even bosses need love. If you harm Mother Nature, she lashes out with floods, hurricanes, earthquakes, and more. If you love her, she will love you to the moon and back.

MEDITATION EXERCISE FOR AN EARTH EMPATH

When life is feeling difficult, it's often an indication that you need to ground yourself.

1. Sit down in a sturdy chair and plant your feet firmly on the ground. Place your hands on your knees with your palms facing up to the sky. Close your eyes and take a few deep breaths.

2. As you breathe, imagine your spine is a tree trunk. See the tree at the base of your spine, encompassing your legs and traveling down into the earth. The roots of the tree extend deeper and deeper until you reach the

center of the earth, the location of the source of earth energy.

3. Imagine this center as a glowing ball of white light. Allow your roots to wrap around it a few times.

4. Now, imagine your roots traveling back up to you. With each deep breath, imagine you are taking white earth energy into your roots and drawing it up toward your body. You are now accessing earth energy.

5. Imagine the energy flowing up your roots until it reaches your feet. See it travel up through your body until it reaches the top of your head, the crown chakra. Then imagine it flowing out of the top of your head like a water fountain.

6. Allow all or some of this energy to cycle from your head to your feet and back down to the center of the earth. Do this three times. You are now grounded.

If you need a quick emergency grounding, go outside and hug a tree. Yes, really.

PROTECTION EXERCISE FOR AN EARTH EMPATH

1. Look around for five items of the same color and focus on them.

2. Look around for four things you can hear and focus on them.

3. Look around for three things you can smell and focus on them.

4. Look around for two things you can touch and focus on them.

5. Look around and find one thing you can taste and
focus on it.

ESSENTIAL OILS FOR AN EARTH EMPATH

Never use essential oils directly on the skin. Always dilute essential
oils with a carrier oil like almond oil, grapeseed oil, coconut oil,
or olive oil. Essential oils are incredibly concentrated. A few drops
are generally all that is needed. Practice aromatherapy by diffusing
essential oils or sprinkling a few drops on a handkerchief or pillow.

- **Rose:** Rose essential oil can help relieve stress and
  boost energy to increase happiness.

CRYSTALS FOR AN EARTH EMPATH

Empaths are sensitive and very intuitive. Because of this, the empath
absorbs both positive and negative energies from other people and
their surroundings. Empaths naturally want to take care of people,
and they often become drained in body, mind, and soul as a result.
Crystals are an amazing tool to help. The best crystals for empaths
protect the energy field (sometimes called an aura), shield an empath
from negative emotions, and keep the empath grounded. You can
wear these crystals as a piece of jewelry, put them in your purse or
pocket, or lay them near you.

- **Citrine:** Citrine represents the sun that shines down to
  the heart of the earth. It balances negative energy and
  shifts it into positive energy to rejuvenate the spirit.

- **Sunstone:** This stone clears away limitations and negative energies by replacing them with light and high vibrations.

AFFIRMATIONS FOR AN EARTH EMPATH

- I feel rooted and stable like a tree.
- I release what isn't mine.
- I always carry positive energy with me.
- It is safe for me to share my authentic self with the world.

SIX
The Child Empath

IS YOUR CHILD AN EMPATH?

1. Does your child feel deeply?

2. Is your child a deep thinker?

3. Is your child sometimes seen as depressed?

4. Does your child have anxiety?

5. Is your child sensitive? Do they sometimes cry when overstimulated?

6. Is your child considered shy or introverted?

7. Does your child have a hard time reading or viewing sad or scary scenes in books, movies, and television shows?

8. Does your child dislike large gatherings?

9. Is your child intuitive?

10. Does your child offer adult-like advice?

11. Is your child a good listener?

12. Is your child compassionate?

13. Is your child overstimulated by loud noises?

14. Is your child afraid of storms?

15. Is your child overstimulated by stress?

16. Is your child sensitive to textures?

17. Is your child sensitive to tastes?

18. Is your child a daydreamer?

19. Does your child fight for the underdog?

20. Does your child often feel different, or as if they don't fit in?

21. Does your child have a strong connection to nature?

22. Does your child have a strong connection to animals?

23. Does your child love stuffed animals?

24. Does your child know when someone is in pain, physical and/or emotional?

25. Does your child adapt well to playing alone?

26. Is your child often seen as an old soul?

27. Does your child act out when emotions or stress are heightened around them?

28. Is your child often seen as overly emotional?

If your child has several of these characteristics, they may be an empath. Empaths—whether they are children or adults—have many synchronized traits.

Please note that the information in this chapter is by no means a replacement for medical or psychiatric help.

SEEK OUT AN EMPATH EXPERT

One of the most common terms used for a child empath is *old soul*. Although there are differences between being an old soul and an empath, most empaths are old souls—but not all old souls are empaths. Children that are old souls are often seen as outcasts. They are sometimes antisocial, so they obviously stand out. They have trouble fitting in with kids their age, and they would rather hang out with adults, communicating the wisdom and experience of an adult themselves.

Being a child empath can be challenging, especially if neither of the child's parents are empaths themselves. It might be overlooked or excused away. Just as you may birth or adopt a child who is a piano prodigy or a child who is amazing at baseball, you would want to foster that gift, right? The same goes for the gift of being an empath.

Being an empath at any age is rarely easy, but children who are empaths are often called all sorts of names from needy to oversensitive to over-emotional and everything in between. None of those terms are helpful, loving, or supportive. When we are misunderstood as children, it can psychologically affect us into adulthood. So, when Great-Aunt Margie calls your infant an old soul or an empath, listen. It's important to provide support for children who have this trait.

Some educators will see that a child has this trait. Some educators will dismiss it. Some educators may be annoyed by it. Empathic children often need help and support when dealing with overwhelming emotions, and if you don't treat their needs sensitively, it can be extremely easy to make them feel worse rather than better. This is why it is crucial to talk to someone who can help the parent and the child deal with being an empath, which might include a therapist or educator.

PARENTING AN EMPATH

Here are some tips for parenting a child empath.

- **Don't lie.** Child empaths pick up on everything, including subtle shifts in body language, emotion, and atmosphere. And when lies are being told, it hurts them on a level only an empath can understand.

- **Don't dismiss their feelings.** If the child empath is feeling sad for "no reason," don't dismiss that emotion. Let them feel their feelings and help them talk about how they are feeling, even if doesn't make sense to you.

- **Be open.** Of course, it's important to be age-appropriate, but it's never worthwhile to try to hide problems from a child empath. They will know something is wrong and is being hidden from them, and they will fear the worst. They may also blame themselves. Reassure them that you are taking care of any problems. Try not to talk to a child empath about adult situations that will cause them more worry.

- **Don't dismiss their physical symptoms.** Many child empaths suffer from headaches, stomachaches, and other physical symptoms. Don't dismiss these symptoms. Instead, show them sympathy and offer support. If they are a hugger, offer them a hug.

- **Allow them to be responsible.** This is a balancing act because you should let a kid be a kid, but empaths want to be helpful, and they like to make others happy with their helpfulness. Encourage their responsibility without requiring it.

- **Encourage them to play.** Show a child empath how to play and play along with them, demonstrating that even adults need playtime to combat responsibilities and stress.

- **Trust them.** If your child is stressed when playing with someone or offers you intuitive information about someone, trust them. You should always listen to a child empath's intuition.

- **Embrace what makes them unique.** Foster the idea that there's nothing wrong with being weird or different.

- **Encourage self-expression.** Let them express themselves, whether that might be through words, art, writing, music, sports, or the clothes they wear. Obviously, make sure their self-expression is done in a respectful way.

- **Create a safe space.** Child empaths need a comfortable spot where they can relax and ground themselves. If they share a bedroom with a sibling, find a space that they can call their own, even if just a corner where they keep their own pillows and toys.

"JUMP HIGHER"

As a child, I had most child empath traits. My stomach would hurt when stress was high in my house. I would run fevers without any reason. I would throw tantrums where I stomped my feet and jumped up and down. "Jump higher," my parents and siblings would laugh, making me jump higher out of frustration. It wasn't funny—it was painful. I didn't know how to express what was happening within me, so I tried to express my feelings through tantrums.

Because I shared a room with my sister, my escape became a small closet in my mom and dad's room. I would close the slatted closet door and cry it out until I either felt better or fell asleep.

If a child empath throws a tantrum or isn't paying attention, this likely isn't them being disrespectful. They may be struggling to process their emotions. Help them find a healthy way to reset by talking about their emotions or encouraging them to ground themselves in a safe space.

EMPATH OVERLOAD SIGNS

- Unexplained tantrums
- Teenage-like moodiness
- Extreme shifts in behavior
- Being emotionally distant
- Shutting down
- Having difficulty focusing
- Excessive shyness
- Avoidant behavior

HELP THEM UNDERSTAND

You might feel in the dark with how to handle your child empath. There are lots of parenting handbooks, but every child and every situation is different. There are outlines and gauges, but parenting a child empath is not a one-size-fits-all. One helpful tactic when parenting a child empath is to teach them that energy matches energy.

If a child empath comes across as difficult or moody and you react with annoyance, they will then match that energy with anger, more moodiness, and possibly disobedience. So how can you help them understand that energy matches energy? Point it out. Have you ever seen a customer get angry at a clerk? The clerk is trained to not match that energy and to stay professional. That's not always the case, and sometimes the clerk lashes back. Use this sort of experience as an opportunity to teach. Show your child videos of customer/clerk interactions or role-play silly scenarios such as "I didn't order pickles on my burger." How would you react as the clerk? How should you react as the customer? See how your child reacts and use this as a teaching moment. Don't dismiss their emotions, but provide guidance in a loving way.

Help your child understand that an empath can feel unstable for no known reason. Empaths will tell you they feel responsible for holding everything together and will take the fall for any faults. But an empath must learn when to set things down and walk away. If they need to take a friend break, okay. If they need to go to bed at 8:00 p.m. or stay in bed until noon, okay. If they want to eat ice cream for dinner, okay. (Or maybe not okay…Until they are an adult, at least.) A child's empath wings are still being formed, and it's important to help them grow.

TEACH COPING SKILLS

Child empaths need healthy emotional coping skills so they can better care for their emotions as they grow into adults. Some examples of coping skills would be:

- **Asking for Space:** Child empaths are forced to be around children of different energy levels in school, often without choice. Child empaths do not like crowds or being around too many people; they might need to do something solitary.

- **Saying No:** No isn't a bad word. I had a relative who refused to let her kids hear the word no because it didn't emphasize the yes in life. I got it, but the word no can't—and shouldn't—be obliterated from our vocabulary. If someone is doing something wrong to a child, the child should learn how to say no. The more child empaths learn that saying no isn't a bad thing, the less exhausted adult empaths we'll see. Limits are okay.

- **Stepping Away:** Teach a child empath that they aren't weak if they decide to step away if the energy is too stressful. It's okay to take a break and try again.

- **Adjusting Expectations:** Remind child empaths that not everyone will be their friend, and that doesn't necessarily mean anything is wrong with them.

- **Meditating:** Meditation doesn't have to be sitting in a dark room with chimes playing. A child empath could meditate while outside catching tadpoles, learning embroidery, knitting, crocheting, baking bread, and so on. As long as the activity is one that relaxes them and helps them connect to their center, they are meditating.

- **Relaxation Techniques:** Things like daydreaming, breathing exercises, blowing bubbles, guided imagery, prayer, etc., are all helpful for child empaths.

- **Drinking Water:** Teach a child empath to stay hydrated. It keeps the brain from feeling sluggish.

- **Focusing on Joy:** Even when a child empath is in a bad mood, try to pivot the energy into something highly vibrational. Ask them questions such as "What funny thing happened today?" or "Can you tell me something that made you smile today?"

- **Napping:** Naps are healthy! Sometimes a nap is the best time-out for the body, mind, and spirit.

- **Moving Around:** Teach a child empath that moving your body boosts circulation, muscle strength, and endorphin production, helping your body work more efficiently.

- **Creating a Vision Board:** Help a child empath create a vision board. This encourages them to dream big.

- **Grounding Themselves:** When a child empath is overwhelmed, encourage them to play in nature. Walk around barefoot, garden, or lie down in the grass and look at the clouds.

- **Relaxing in a Bath or Shower:** Relaxing in the bath or shower can be a great way for a child empath to wash away the negative energies of the day.

While being a child is difficult for most, being a child empath can also be confusing. The more aware parents of child empaths are, the more they can help a child empath grow into a mature and healthy adult who can effectively manage their gift.

COMFORT THE INNER CHILD

It's not surprising that many empaths were wounded children, hoarding an array of emotions from their childhood. That whirlwind of emotion—usually including feelings of grief, rejection, and abandonment—is often awoken in adulthood to be tended to. Empaths are deep feelers, and that inner child needs to be loved as deeply as they love others.

SING A SONG

I had heard the rumors about the third-grade teacher since I was in kindergarten. He was mean. He hit you with a paddle if you gave a wrong answer. And he swore at the class in German. I was petrified. By this time in my life, my mom had been in and out of the mental hospital several times, and days before I was to start third grade, I lost my person—my grandfather.

My grandfather, my mother's dad, was a gentle and loving man who'd lost his wife and two sons in a short span of time. Even though he suffered tragedies, he was a calming influence on my household with every visit, and he visited frequently. He would often pick me up from school in his large boat of a car. I'd sit in the passenger seat with the seatbelt swallowing me. With one hand on the steering wheel and the other with his lit Marlboro, he'd ask me about my day. On one of the last days of second grade, I had confessed my fear of going into third grade because of the teacher.

"I'll never let him hurt you, Kristy," he told me. "I'll protect you," he promised, setting his cigarette down and squeezing my hand tight.

But then my grandfather passed away, and I was left to face this scary teacher while grieving my bodyguard and best friend. My mom was sympathetic, but I needed to go to school, and since this was a small parochial school, there was only one teacher per grade. So, there was no way out of the situation—I was stuck with this teacher.

"I'll go to jail if you don't go to school, Kristy," my mom scolded as we walked to school on my first day. She held her unlit cigarette between her fingers for the half-mile walk, not taking a puff.

Her hard words added more stress to the mountain of stress I was already feeling. I didn't say anything during the walk, otherwise the faucet of tears would start and never stop. I wanted to have a tantrum. I wanted to beg. But I knew nothing would change the ultimate outcome.

As we neared the schoolyard, I looked down, kicking the white stones and dirtying my new tennis shoes. I cringed, waiting for my mom to yell at me with a side eye. She didn't, but I furiously willed for a superpower of invisibility because right then, we were standing near the scary teacher. It was then that my tears began to fall—hard.

"This must be Krissy," the teacher commented as my mom continued to drag me even closer to the school door.

The tears continued to stain my face and instead of wiping them, I gripped my mom's hand harder. I continued looking down, staring at the teacher's dark black dress shoes, awed that there was no dust on them even though the parking lot was all gravel. I could see my shoes too, so my wish of invisibility was rendered void.

My mom didn't correct him on my name. Instead, she tried explaining my tears. "We just buried my dad, her grandpa," she told him instead of mentioning the fact that I was also scared of him, obvious by my tight hold on her hand.

"It's okay, Krissy." The teacher's tone was soft and understanding, nothing like I'd imagined. "She'll be okay," he told my mom, taking my hand firmly from my mom's and leading me into the school. We walked to my new classroom and to my desk, which had my name—KRISTY—written on it.

Everything I had heard about that teacher turned out to be true. He swore in German, which made the parents less than thrilled. Kids hear and kids repeat. But honestly, most of the parents were afraid of this teacher as well, so nothing was ever said. If the class wasn't listening, if someone in the class didn't do an assignment properly, or if the teacher was simply angry, he would scream out "*Dummkopf*," which means idiot/stupid person in German. There was nothing like negative energy to perpetuate the negatives in my already-complicated childhood. Kids did get paddled, but I kept my head down and was as quiet as I could be to avoid being noticed. Then one day, my teacher asked to meet with me after school.

"Krissy, I believe you are talented. I want to hear you sing."

I just stared at him with a blank look. This teacher was also the church's organist and music director. He was a gifted pianist and his voice, like his energy, was a deep and booming bass.

"I want you to sing, Krissy," he repeated, a bit firmer.

I looked around to see if anyone was there, but we were alone. He sat down at the small piano, handed me sheet music with words on it, and began to play, pointing at me for the cue. And I sang. And my teacher smiled.

"It's decided. I want you to sing in the talent show." He got up and left the room, leaving me to figure out what had just happened.

After that day, I would rush home from school, do my homework, and spend the rest of the evening practicing my singing. I would love to tell you a happily ever after about how I was discovered by a talent scout after the show, but not so much. I ended up doing a song with friends, and I can't even tell you what we sang. (In fact, I texted one of my childhood friends to ask while writing this and she couldn't remember either.) All I remember is practicing relentlessly at recess. That talent show, though, opened something within me. I began taking dancing lessons, I tried out for *Annie* on Broadway (a sad tale of humiliating rejection), I started percussion lessons, I never stopped singing, and I was coming into my own voice (no pun intended). Yes, I was only in third grade—and here I am now, in my fifties, still discovering who I am—but music became my outlet for all my feelings and the feelings I felt from others. I could pour my emotions into a song, its lyrics, and the music. I could pound it out with my drumsticks. I could belt out my grief. And I could also express my happiness through music.

Decades later, I took my husband to the school grounds to show him where I went to school. The neighborhood around the school had become dicey in the decades since I was there, so things looked different, but as soon as I stepped foot onto the property, memories came flooding back. Chuck and I took a seat on the grass. In the quiet, I allowed the good, the bad, and the ugly feelings of those years to swirl around. Then a van pulled up, with a frail elderly man in the driver's seat.

"What are you doing here?" the man barked at us. Then a hint of recognition flashed in his eyes. "Krissy? Is that you?"

This teacher was the only person in the world that ever called me "Krissy"—or, at least, the only person who I allowed to call me "Krissy." I blinked back the tears that began to spring to my eyes.

"It is," I softly answered, standing up and walking over to the vehicle's window. It had been well over thirty years since I'd seen this man.

"It's good to see you, Krissy. I'm not sure you heard, but I lost my daughter to breast cancer not long ago."

I hadn't heard, but I nodded and listened as he poured his heart out. He talked about his kids, his daughter's passing, and how he didn't know how to fully retire even though he wanted to. It was surreal to be counseling the man I was so afraid of all those years ago, but there we were. I didn't tell him what I was doing professionally. He didn't ask. It didn't matter; he just needed someone to listen to him.

After we finished talking, he smiled crookedly and said, "It was good to see you. I always saw something special in you. You were always sensitive." He said it as a compliment, though.

We said our goodbyes and I quietly walked back and sat beside my husband. Then the tears fell. Because the memories that flooded back... Not many of them were good. It brought up my grief for my grandpa and for my mom. It brought up my feelings of inadequacy as a kid. It brought up a lot. So, I did what I do best: I cried. It was a healing cry, though, because unlike what non-empaths try to preach, tears *are* healing. I had no idea I'd stored all that grief and sadness in my emotional attic or that it needed to be released.

Because I understood what it was like to be an empath, I thought I was prepared to be a parent to an empath. Uh, yeah, about that...

EMPATHS IN THE WOMB

For some child empaths, their gift is like putting on a shoe that is too big: they must eventually grow into it. Other child empaths are born with shoes that fit perfectly right from the get-go. Not all empaths are created equal. Not only do empaths have different traits, but they also they aren't all warm, fuzzy, and loving. Some have a tough time deciphering their gift and instead try to ignore it and push it away; they may even begin doing this during childhood.

The empath gift is confusing to kids and adults alike. Many adults see the gift as a sign of weakness and tears a sign of being too sensitive. But the more information adults are armed with, the more we can help future generations manage depression, anxiety, low self-worth, and lack of confidence. Not everyone will want to understand empathy, but knowledge will always be power. And adults often misunderstand the empath gift, like my daughter's first-grade teacher did.

I decided as soon as I found out I was going to be a mom that I wanted to be a cool mom. I was going to listen to classical music while pregnant. I wasn't going to eat or drink anything that was considered even slightly bad for the baby. Once I was given a caffeinated pop rather than a decaffeinated pop. Even though I noticed after taking one small sip, I thought for sure my child would be damaged for the rest of her life. That didn't happen, thankfully, but this was my first child, and I put a lot of unrealistic expectations on myself and on her.

When I found out the baby was a girl, I conjured more unrealistic expectations. She would wear twirly pink princess dresses. She'd love makeup like I do. She'd take dancing classes and be a cheerleader. We would do one another's nails, cook together, eat cookie dough together, and be the real-life Lorelei and Rory Gilmore of the witty television show *Gilmore Girls*. Truth be told, that did end up being the case, but not until Micaela left for college and came home kinda liking me—*kinda*. Before that, if I dared buy her anything pink, the eye roll was intense. Nail polish or makeup? Not unless it was gothic and dark. Her clothing preferences were far from princess, tutu, or even floral. Instead, she liked shabby, vampire-like capes, crazy knee-high socks, and Dr. Martens, or anything from Hot Topic. Her mood matched her black lipstick. She was my little thundercloud that felt everything, hiding behind a book or a snarky, disgusted look (which was always sent my way).

I respected her choices, but for years I felt like I didn't know who the young lady living under my own roof was. It felt like she only thought of me as the prison warden holding all the keys. She was the soul I had grown for nine months, sang to, played music for, and prayed for, and I felt we could both learn from one another. As I look back, I can say we both did learn from one another, and we grew because of the good, the bad, and the ugly.

Oh, and there was a lot of ugly.

Micaela was a colicky baby. Even though the doctor said she wasn't allergic to anything, I now realize she was allergic to the stress in the house. Then I got pregnant just a few months after having her, which resulted in emergency surgery and a "you'll likely never get pregnant again" from the doctor. Waking up from said surgery to find my then-husband flirting with the nurse made me not want to get pregnant again anyhow. That's the interesting thing about empaths—empaths are forgivers. Two years later I welcomed another baby into the world, this time a baby boy born deaf and with a cleft palate. I spent my time dashing between doctor appointments and fighting off depression, because another empath quality is to absorb blame, even when there's no blame to be dished out and eaten. I blamed myself for *everything*. It didn't help that a pimply young resident had come into my hospital room right after hearing the news of Connor's cleft and asked me what drugs I took while pregnant.

"You had to take *something*," he emphasized with a pause and a stare, "to give your child a birth defect!"

Had I taken a Tylenol before I knew I was pregnant? Maybe I had some cough medicine before I knew I was pregnant? Oh no, maybe a drink of caffeine? No, I didn't think I had, but even if I had, it was an unfair guilt trip that turned out to be very expensive and didn't lead to any sunshine, spas, or surf either. In the end, Connor was fine. His cleft was repaired before his first birthday and his hearing loss is now merely male selective hearing.

By the time Micaela started kindergarten, though, I was amid a messy divorce with her father. One day she refused to put on her ballet slippers for the class that she had loved so much just a few weeks before, and let's just say I wasn't the cool mom I had hoped I'd be. I was a mess. And Micaela felt it even if I didn't say a single word. Connor felt it too, but they felt things differently. Connor would climb in my lap and offer me a hug or ask for quiet time with a book. Micaela, on the other hand, would slap me across the face with just a look. I can laugh about it now, but at the time I was devastated. Micaela fought me on everything. I had failed her—or so I thought.

First grade was difficult for Micaela, and our already-toxic home only caused more issues. Along with the divorce and adjusting to the "this house, that house" juggle of co-parenting, Micaela's first-grade teacher wasn't the kindhearted type. Instead of having compassion for the changes in our lives, Micaela's teacher would physically yank her into the hallway and tell her to cry there. The teacher would tell Micaela that when she got herself together, she could come back to the classroom. Being a feeler was an inconvenience to this teacher. Micaela's second-grade teacher, though, understood and offered me understanding too.

One day after school I opened Micaela's school locker to find it an embarrassing mess, from old food wrappers to paper bags. She was like a ninety-year-old hoarder of this and that. "Just throw it out!" I'd nag. Little did I knew that her locker was one of the things she felt she could control. It wasn't at my house or her dad's house—it was *hers*. But because I thought it was a reflection of me, I started grabbing all her miscellaneous "treasures" and tossing them into the garbage.

"Mom!" she yelped when she saw what I was doing. She knelt in front of the trash and carefully pulled out the garbage, holding it close to her as if it were a stuffed animal or doll I'd tossed. "Don't!" she cried.

Her second-grade teacher came out of the classroom to see what all the commotion was about. I was crying. Micaela was crying.

"Let's talk," she said to me, gently grabbing my arm and leading me to a quiet alcove.

"I'm sorry," I began. "I know she's still having a hard time with the divorce—"

The teacher cut me off. "She's fine, Kristy. I think it's you that might not be."

How dare she! She doesn't know anything about me. I could feel the blood rushing to my face. I dug my nails into my palms to keep myself from standing there and sobbing out of anger and shame.

"That girl there," the teacher pointed to Micaela, "is one of the sweetest I've ever taught. You helped with that. She's creative. Quirky. Different. She's compassionate and empathic. Her tears aren't a bother and shouldn't be treated as such."

Tell your coworker that! I wanted to scream, but I listened.

"Let me tell you what happened the other day. I woke up on the wrong side of the bed. I was upset about everything. My husband and I got into a tiff, and then I got a phone call that my mom had been rushed to the hospital. I came to work with a load on my shoulders. I'm good with my poker face, but apparently your daughter sees through all of that. She walked into the classroom and looked hard at me, as if she was seeing every emotion inside of me and not just my facial expressions. She walked over to my desk and asked if she could give me a hug. She'd never done that before.

"I know I have a reputation for being tough. I've been called mean. I have a tough exterior, but your daughter saw through all that to try and help *me* feel better. I accepted the hug, went to the bathroom, cried, and restarted my day. Kristy, if her room is dirty, shut the door. I'm not saying stop parenting, but give her some freedom to be her, because she's a beautiful person. If she wants to collect aluminum foil, well, let her!"

I wanted to interject with *What about rodents or mice or dirt or...*I didn't. I got her point. She was saying to choose my battles. I wanted to ask why Micaela could feel *her* pain and sadness and try to take it away, yet wanted to add to mine, but that would be for my own discovery. Those of us with kids know that kids behave better outside of their own home, and it is what is taught within the home that makes them do that.

THE FUNERALS

Funerals are hard for everyone, empath or not. The intense tsunami of emotions that funerals create can be confusing. And for a child who is an empath, they can be incredibly soul stirring. Parents of a child empath can decide whether their child should attend a funeral or not, and how long they should stay at the funeral if they do attend; there are no right or wrong answers. However, a child empath attending a funeral for any amount of time can make them an unwilling sponge to unfair energy. Until the child empath learns how to cleanse that energy—or until a parent can help them cleanse that energy—this can be an uncomfortable situation for everyone.

Years ago, Micaela's great-grandmother passed away after a bout with cancer. She was a lovely lady; she tried to teach me how to knit and crochet (with much patience), and she loved on every one of her children, grandchildren, and great-grandchildren with strength and a firm chin. Now, it was her time to rest.

"I really think she's too young to go," I said, packing up the diaper bag.

"She's so young that she won't even know. Plus, we don't have a babysitter. Our babysitters will be at the funeral," my daughter's father said flatly.

Micaela was only about two years old, but I still wasn't thrilled about bringing her to the funeral. I just had a feeling. Call it mother's intuition or empath intuition, but I was right. Micaela behaved just fine at the funeral, but not long after she turned feverish. *Probably a tooth coming in*, we tried to reason. *Maybe a virus*, we thought when no tooth popped through; after all, there had been so many people at the funeral. There were a lot of assumptions about what could be wrong, but I knew all too well Micaela was suffering from energy overload, and sort of like a virus, it had to run its course. I decided that a calming bath with lavender, some snuggles, and plenty of sleep would help Micaela bounce back from energy overload. And she did.

As a parent, we try to shield our children from stressful situations. A child empath is attuned to every slight shift in the environment. Much like a boat unanchored during a storm, things may be fine once the storm has resolved, or the boat might be treading water. Throwing my empathic infant into the energy that a funeral gives off wasn't the best of ideas.

THE NEXT FUNERAL

Children do not have control over most things in their life, and for child empaths, factor in the inability to control empath energy. Being an empath can feel like being a radio whose volume continues to get turned up louder and louder, and no one is able to find the knob to turn it down. Energy is loud. Words say one thing, but energy screams something else. Empath energy isn't like a monster under the bed: it's real and true energy, and it can affect everyone in the household. Empath energy takes feelers prisoner unless they know how to navigate it.

When I began to understand my own empath gift in my early thirties, I realized I could help my children work through their own gifts. The methods I used to manage my empath gift came with a lot of judgment, though. In the late '90s and early 2000s, meditation, crystals, smoke cleansing, and other holistic modalities were considered hippieish and new age, practices that were only done by granola-crunching people. Maybe these methods are still considered hippieish to many, but they helped me navigate my emotions—and they continue to help.

My mom lost her sight when I was twelve years old. Along with her blindness, she had an array of autoimmune diseases. Then, in 2005, she had a heart attack. Her arteries were too narrow to do a stent of any kind, so the doctors tried medication to clear up the blockage. In January of 2006, she had another heart attack. This time, the doctors wanted to do open-heart surgery. It was one of those *If we don't do the surgery she will die, and if we do the surgery she will likely die, but maybe she won't, but probably* situations. So, we tried the surgery. It landed Mom in the cardiac care unit for several weeks.

At the time, I was working in the corporate field, trying very hard to find my way out. My coworkers were difficult, and my boss couldn't figure me out. I was "too nice" for him. I was "too peppy" for him. I was "too much" for him—another thing empaths are often accused of and belittled for. I never complained about my job to my kids, but they knew I was unhappy.

At work, I tried hard to keep my personal life personal, but because of the frequent phone calls from my mother's doctor and my father during work hours, I had to fill my boss in on my mom's health failing. I also requested time off for her surgery. I gave no reason for him to doubt me, but it was his nature to be suspicious. Although he approved my time off, I overheard my boss telling the office manager that he thought I was likely interviewing for a new job and that my mom wasn't sick.

It was just a couple of days before my mother's passing when my mom's nurse called me to tell me my boss had called to check on the status of my mom. Of course, the nurse didn't give him any status because it wasn't his business, but she wanted me to know. I had never once given him or anyone else in that establishment a reason to distrust me. I was appalled. Here I was, going to work during the day and sitting by my mother's bedside at night, and my boss didn't believe me. Again, I didn't mention this to the kids, but they knew.

When I sat by my mother's bedside at night, I did it alone. I wouldn't let my kids see my mom in the hospital. She was on a ventilator and dying; it was too much for me. Micaela was eleven and Connor was eight, and even though they didn't see my mom at the end, they are empaths, so they felt more than I wanted them to. To this day, I'm unsure if I made the right decision to not give them that goodbye, but I know my mother wouldn't have wanted them to see her that way.

When my mother passed away after several weeks in the cardiac care unit, I picked my kids up from their father's house, and without even saying anything, I knew they knew. I'm sure my mascara-stained face also gave hints.

My boss and coworkers came to my mom's visitation, which I still think was very kind of them. When he saw my boss, Connor took his hand and led him to my mom's casket.

"Do you believe my mom now?" he sassed. "Do you believe my grandma was ill now, now that she's dead?"

My boss booked it out of the funeral home as fast as he could. As much as I wanted to ask my son where he had gotten his information, I didn't. As much as I wanted to scold my son for being disrespectful to my boss, I didn't do that either. It was my son's way of nobly protecting me and his grandmother.

My daughter, the one who cried over everything, had pulled up a chair next to my mother's casket and was dutifully holding her hand. With her shoulders back, Micaela wiped away her tears before they fell. She acted as my mother's guardian because "Nana is probably scared."

I was better prepared for this funeral than I was for the one that Micaela attended as an infant; I knew that Micaela, Connor, and I needed to cleanse ourselves after the service so that none of us suffered from energy overload. After the funeral luncheon, we went home, and I had everybody change into pajamas. Then I turned on a comedy. We ate junk food. I lit yummy-smelling candles. We told silly stories of my mom. And we laughed. This wasn't done out of disrespect; it was so the sad and depressive energy didn't cling to us like saran wrap in a rainstorm. Grief has a way of doing that to an empath.

KIDS NEED TO UNPLUG TOO

If something isn't working, usually you just need to unplug it for a while—including yourself. I loved naps as a baby, and I still love them. Naps and meditation are forms of unplugging. They serve as a reset, and kids need to learn how to unplug too so that when they become adults, it is second nature.

When I took a child psychology class during college, I was required to have an internship. My internship took place at the college's child development center. I was supposed to observe and participate as well. I've always loved children, especially three- and four-year-olds, and I was lucky to get that internship. Together, the children and I sang, played music, colored, and did puzzles, and I observed free time, lunch, and nap time.

According to my colleagues, there was one boy who was challenging. Joshua didn't want to sit with anyone, share, or participate, and during nap time he ran around all the kids, causing conflict. The more the teachers and assistants reacted, the more he acted up. It was a vicious cycle. You could tell the other employees didn't like this child because he was high-maintenance. I could tell he felt unliked, which made him upset, so the cycle continued.

My colleagues had talks with his mother, who was concerned. Joshua had been a good boy at home, but she'd gone back to work after her divorce, so he had to go to day care, where he was bad all day, every day. What a stigma to have as a three-year-old! I asked the teachers if I could try something. I was a green college student, but I think they were desperate enough that they didn't care.

"Joshua," I said to him. "It's going to be nap time soon, so I want you to think about where you want your nap mat to go."

Joshua gave me the strangest look. Normally during nap time, the kids were told to find a spot and lie down, but Joshua just ran around causing ruckus. He'd never had to choose a spot for his nap mat.

A few minutes later it was nap time, and I asked Joshua where he chose to put his mat. He sheepishly pointed to a corner far from all the other kids, nearest the coat closet.

"What an excellent choice! Okay, grab your mat," I said.

"But that's not where we nap," one of the little girls contested.

The teacher shh'd her and corralled the other kids to their napping spots, while Joshua carefully laid his mat down and lay on top of it. Within a minute, he was fast asleep. It seemed Joshua had a hard time in crowds. Being told to rest in the middle of all the kids was stressful for him. He also appreciated being given a choice.

Before long, he was moving his mat closer and closer to the other kids. He wasn't a problem child, he was simply going through a lot at home and was also thrust into a whole lot of energy at day care.

Some people feel the need to try and compartmentalize the energy in a room by being on the edge of it. Do you or someone you know have to sit in the aisle seat at church, the movie theater, or anywhere else you are sitting in a row? When you choose an aisle seat, you have all that energy to one side of you but feel a space on the other side. It's not weird—it's an empath trait.

THE TEENAGE EMPATH

Teenagers face many challenges, including navigating relationships with their peers. Unkind words hurt, and an empath hangs on to each word. They play those words over and over. Unkind words haunt a teenage empath, poisoning their confidence, their self-worth, and their soul. The teenage empath hears all sorts of things through energy. It's not always the words said, but the energy felt: "You suck!" "I don't love you anymore." "I am so disappointed in you." "You are ugly!" "You aren't talented." Negative energy can cause grudges and lead to an array of emotions that continue to play with the teen empath's mind and heart. This can stop a teen from wanting to love, try new things, and grow into their own. It's no wonder a lot of teenage empaths escape into their own world! They become like a butterfly stuck in a mason jar, unable to experience the world. The teen empath may still be a child, but they have big feelings. They want to be understood and heard, but they find it confusing to share their feelings. Because of this, feelings might express themselves as eye rolls or stormy moods.

When I was a teenager, my high school held a fundraiser each year just before Valentine's Day. For the fundraiser, you could buy a carnation and write a small note to attach to it, and the flower and note would be delivered during homeroom on Valentine's Day. I would always save up and send carnations to my friends, all the while secretly hoping that I'd receive a carnation from a secret admirer. Recently, a friend from high school mentioned this experience and said, "I never received any, and I'm still mad at y'all." All my memories about the Valentine's Day fundraiser came flooding back. I also never received any carnations. One year on Valentine's Day, I was so anxious about receiving or not receiving flowers that my mom let me stay home. I was trying to anticipate the letdown, but all it did was make me more depressed.

Children and adult empaths are the wounded healers. I felt so unworthy in that situation, and although my mom let me stay home from school that day as an escape rather than a lesson, my mom did what she thought was best. Teenage empaths will get their feelings hurt. They won't be invited to a party; they will be dumped by someone they loved. Teaching teenage empaths not to devalue themselves by trying to prove they are worthy of love is important. Then, when teenage empaths become adults, they will know that they are worthy of love just as they are.

FORCED FAMILY FUN

The days and nights can be filled with so much to do, especially once you have children. The world becomes a spinning calendar full of appointments and events, and we must consciously choose how we spend our moments. Child empaths crave spending time with their loved ones and making memories, but they may not know how to communicate that. They may even complain, but as they grow, they will treasure the silly pictures and experiences.

I never remember saying I wanted to be a mommy, yet I knew I wanted to have children. Nobody is prepared to become a parent, no matter how much they prepare. When I think back to the time I held my firstborn in my arms, I think about what a child I was at twenty-three years old. Even though I had babysat before, I had no idea what to do and what not to do under certain circumstances.

There is no one-size-fits-all parenting manual, as every child is different and demands a different parenting style. Micaela would throw tantrums as soon as I tried to get her into a car seat. Her screams were so fierce and loud it was as if I was murdering her. Then came Connor, who was calm and patient. Micaela started walking at six months of age, which was a nightmare with baby-proofing and trying to keep her in the crib that she endlessly climbed out of. Connor took his first steps on his first birthday. Micaela liked her room messy and wore mismatched socks and rumpled shirts without apology. Since the beginning of time, Connor liked everything color coordinated and in order. Every child is different, but joyful just the same. (Yes, even during teething, colic, and curfew feuds.)

Because I was a single mom for so long, I spent a lot of time just trying to pay for the roof over our heads by working full-time and part-time jobs and going to college. But I knew how important quality time was, especially for child empaths, so I created "Forced Family Fun Fridays." When the kids were little, we would do something every other week, but as they got older, we became a blended family with two more kids, and their schedules were fuller, so it was more like once a month and/or during school breaks. We didn't do anything spectacular on Forced Family Fun Friday—it could be playing a game of Yahtzee, going to the movies, laser tag, visiting a museum, etc.—but we tried to make it as magical as possible. Everybody offered suggestions, which we kept in a fishbowl, but most of the time one (or all) of the kids would complain about the selected activity. In the end, we would laugh and have fun.

Forced Family Fun Friday was a great way for the kids to de-stress —and for us adults too. To reduce stress and foster a healthier empath:

- Make sure everyone is given space when they need it. Alone time is crucial for an empath.
- Everyone needs to pitch in. Everyone.
- Watch your attitude—it's contagious.
- Schedule time together.
- Have a family meeting about responsibilities; don't assume everyone is on the same page.
- Stick to a routine.
- Make time to laugh.
- Watch a comedy together.
- Turn on fun music and dance.
- Talk in different accents during dinner.

SUPERNATURAL KIDS

It's common for child empaths to have supernatural or paranormal experiences. Children are closer to heaven than most, and are purer in nature. They don't have the cultural filters we build as adults. As people grow, we become more jaded, and we often take the saying "There's no such thing as ghosts" to heart. Sometimes it's because of fear, and sometimes it is simply because of a lack of understanding.

The adults who say "There's no such thing as ghosts" aren't necessarily fearful of ghosts, premonitions, or intuitive mentions, but it is a parent's job to protect their child, and sometimes this is the easiest answer. Supernatural situations can be peculiar. Just as there isn't an individualized parenting handbook for each child, there's not a one-size-fits-all manual for supernatural children titled "So Your Kid Knows, Sees, and Senses Things." (That sure would be nice, though.)

Years ago, I was doing a book signing when a young girl came up to my table.

"What are your books about?" she asked me.

I hesitated but decided to be truthful. "Heaven, ghosts, and spirits."

"Are ghosts real?" she asked, outlining the butterfly on one of my book covers with her finger.

Uh. Um. How to answer? I wanted to be truthful, but this was a loaded question. Or was it?

"Yes, ghosts are real," I firmly answered, smiling at her. "But most are friendly," I emphasized.

The little girl turned to her mother, who was hurriedly walking toward my table, apologizing that her daughter was bothering me.

"See, Mom, I told you ghosts were real. This lady says so!"

Oh boy.

"Do ghosts like bananas?" the young girl innocently asked me.

"Well, ghosts don't need to eat, so they might've liked bananas when they were alive."

"Wait," the mother said. "Is this why I keep finding bananas in your closet?"

"Yes," the girl said. "I told you this already. Every night, this man comes out of my closet. He has a long winter coat on with a checkered hat. He looks hungry. You told me bananas are good for you, so I thought maybe he'd like a banana!"

The mom's eyes watered over as she had a reckoning. She turned to me. "She's describing my grandfather. She's actually staying in his room," she whispered. "Oh my. He passed from cancer and was so frail before he died. I should've listened to her more carefully when she was telling me. I thought it was an imaginary friend and it would go away. Do you think…?"

I nodded before she finished her sentence.

The little girl seemed more curious than frightened. Even though her mother had discounted the paranormal event, it didn't dissuade the visits or affect the girl's ability to see the ghost.

This interaction reminded me of when my kids were young and began to see spirits. Once, at bedtime, I was agitated with the repeated "I'm thirsty," "I'm hungry," "Just one more kiss" excuses to delay sleep. Then I heard, "Mom, there's a ghost in my room." I was so annoyed that I almost yelled out "There's no such thing as ghosts!" and had to stop myself. What should I even say? *Yes, there is. They just aren't like Casper the Friendly Ghost.* That's exactly what I told them. Kids are receptive and sensitive in so many ways.

He Sees Dead People

Kids are open to the idea of Santa Claus and the Easter Bunny, making all things possible for them, including the paranormal. Many adults don't even understand the paranormal, so when you add in a child who senses and sees things, it can be confusing for all parties. Child empaths seem to be more open to the paranormal than most, but as they grow, this sometimes changes.

I worked with a family who had a child that was sensitive to the supernatural. As a baby, Zeeland had always waved and giggled at what his parents thought was the air. "Oh look, he's talking to the angels," his mom, Rachel, would say.

"It didn't feel scary then, but when Zee turned three, his toys would turn on when nobody was nearby. It didn't scare him, but it sure did scare us. It was weird," Rachel told me.

Zeeland was still having paranormal experiences at five years old, and the more his parents showed their uncertainty (which sometimes turned into impatience and frustration), the more he reacted. Then he started talking about seeing people in his room. Zeeland didn't want to go to bed alone; he needed one of his parents to sleep with him, or he would climb into bed with them in the middle of the night. They were all exhausted by the time they called me.

One of the first things I asked him was, "Zeeland, can you draw who you see in your room and describe the picture to me as you draw?"

I gave him a large piece of paper and a box of markers and crayons, and Zeeland started drawing.

"This man has round glasses and no hair," he explained. "And this lady, she sometimes brings a baby with her, and she wears a dress with big flowers on it or a white dress," he cheerfully explained, continuing to draw and color.

"Rachel, do you have any photo albums with your grandparents and/or great-grandparents in them?"

Rachel thought for a moment and nodded, holding up one finger for me to wait a moment, and went racing off. When she came back with the photo albums, we explored the photos together. Zeeland stopped us at one photo.

"That is the lady. That's the lady I see!" he smiled and went back to coloring.

I looked at Rachel, who had paled. Instead of questioning, I waited. She said, "That would be my dad's mom. She died in childbirth with my dad's brother. He passed as well. The white dress would be because she was a nurse herself."

We both sat in silence as we processed this.

We never figured out who the male ghost was, but sometimes it's not a relative. Sometimes kids see their guides. Sometimes it's a previous homeowner or someone their parents worked with.

Zeeland is now ten years old and would rather play hockey than talk about spirits and ghosts. "He did know I was pregnant before I did, though," Rachel said, rocking her new baby girl. "But I don't know if it was intuition or if I was extra hormonal," she laughed.

If Your Child Senses the Supernatural…

- Don't discount the information they give you. Sometimes it is a product of a vivid imagination, but not always. Believe them.
- Don't make a big deal about it.
- Don't press them, but ask for more information.
- At nighttime, stay with your child until they are comfortable. This time of day can be frightening for child empaths; the lights are turned off, electronics are turned off, and senses are turned up.
- Put a night-light in your child's room.
- Teach your child an affirmation such as "I am safe."
- Teach your child that they can be assertive with spirits and tell them to go away.
- Create an amulet or other symbol of protection such as a dream catcher, an angel figurine, a special nighttime stuffed animal, etc., that they can keep near their bed.

TOOLS FOR A CHILD EMPATH

There are many steps that a child empath can take to be as healthy and happy as possible. I've included some suggestions for essential oils, crystals, and affirmations, as well as tips and a meditation for children empaths.

NAME THAT FEELING

One of my favorite exercises to help a child empath re-ground themselves is to play in water. *(Never leave a child unattended around water.)* You can play with water in your kitchen sink or during bath time; you could also use a bucket or bowl of water.

When a child empath is feeling overwhelmed, have them spell out how they feel in the water. Ask if they want you to guess, but be respectful if they'd rather you not know. If they can't spell yet, ask them to draw a face in the water as to how they feel (sad, happy, silly, etc.). You can also ask the child if they want to guess how you are feeling; if they do, write or draw in the water for them.

MEDITATION EXERCISES FOR A CHILD EMPATH

This exercise is best done lying on the ground while looking at a sky full of puffy clouds, but it can also be done while sitting in the car or by simply pretending that you are looking at puffy clouds.

1. Be silent and watch the clouds for a while.

2. Say, "Not one cloud is the same. Some clouds move independently, and some form into a larger cloud. Just like humans, no cloud is the same. They are all unique and beautiful. They are always changing and always moving, never staying in the same spot."

3. Continue to watch the clouds.

4. Say, "Thoughts are like clouds, and they move through the mind."

5. Continue to watch the clouds.

6. Say, "If you become distracted by a thought, bring yourself back to the clouds and let it pass through your mind."

7. After a while, say, "Even if the sky is cloudy, eventually a beautiful day appears—just like the thoughts that go through our mind."

8. Take a few deep breaths and continue about your day.

High On a Mountain Meditation

Have a child/teen empath get comfortable. Then read the following steps to them, pausing in between steps:

1. Close your eyes and stretch your arms out on both sides. Picture yourself standing on top of a windy mountain. Feel the wind blowing in your hair and breathe in the fresh air.

2. Slowly look down the mountain at a walking path. Notice how far you've come. See the accomplishments you've made by climbing as high as you have.

3. Look high in the sky at the white, puffy clouds. Notice that they are slowly beginning to form a word. This is your power word. Pay attention to what it is.

4. Breathe deeply and thank yourself for an amazing journey. Take that power word with you as inspiration.

5. Take a deep breath in and out and open your eyes.

PROTECTION TIPS FOR A CHILD EMPATH

Just as children should brush their teeth every morning, child/teen empaths should protect themselves from excess energy every morning.

Have them visualize a bubble of light. They can also visualize the light as a fog or as an astronaut-like suit. The bubble/fog/suit can be any color they like. Then have them say, "This bubble of light only allows love to enter into my presence."

If the child empath is feeling more feelings than they think they should, tell them to simply reenforce the bubble/fog/suit.

Release

If your child/teen empath is feeling all the feelings, have them say out loud or in their head:

Release

Release

Release

Have them continue to say "Release" until they feel like it is time to take a huge sigh and relax. Then have them set an intention related to the reason they were feeling so tense. For example, if they got a bad grade on a test and feel stupid, they could say, "I forgive myself for my mistakes. I am smart. I can start again." If the tension was related to heartbreak, the intention might be, "I deserve loving and supportive people in my life."

ESSENTIAL OILS FOR A CHILD EMPATH

It's not recommended to use essential oils on children. *Always consult your family doctor before using essential oils on children.* For child empaths, I like to use an organic means of essential oils. Simply squeeze a citrus fruit such as an orange, grapefruit, or lemon into a bowl of water, then gently boil the liquid. Citrus scents can help empathic children keep their vibrational energy uplifted.

CRYSTALS FOR A CHILD EMPATH

Empaths are sensitive and very intuitive. Because of this, the empath absorbs both positive and negative energies from other people and their surroundings. Empaths naturally want to take care of people, and they often become drained in body, mind, and soul as a result. Crystals are an amazing tool to help. The best crystals for empaths protect the energy field (sometimes called an aura), shield an empath from negative emotions, and keep the empath grounded. Crystals can be worn as a piece of jewelry, put in a pocket, or laid nearby. *Crystals can be a choking hazard, so keep crystals away from your child until they are old enough to handle them.*

- **Sodalite:** Sodalite helps calm an overactive mind. It helps control emotions and releases any fear, worry, and sadness that a child empath may absorb.

AFFIRMATIONS FOR A CHILD EMPATH

- I am loved. I am loveable. I am love.
- I can do anything I set my mind to.
- I control my own happiness.
- I spread kindness to others, including myself.

SEVEN
Empaths and Love

Once upon a time, there was a group of people who were the caregivers of the world, also known as empaths. The world was happy empaths existed because at one point or another, we all need to be nurtured. But there was also another group. This group looked innocent, and they welcomed the empaths' help with open arms. The problem was, the group was not innocent—they were narcissists. They pretended to be broken and unable to help themselves. Most of the time, the narcissists hung out in their dumpster, which was filled with broken pieces, some very sharp and hurtful. Although the empaths weren't sure they wanted to be there, the core of their being was to fix, to help, and so they sat in the dumpster with the narcissists. Over time, they got used to the abuse. They sacrificed their own happiness. They got cut by the narcissists' broken pieces. And the narcissist never even noticed, because they were busy looking for another person to fix them just in case the empath didn't survive their injuries.

Dumpster diving is dangerous, and it damages an empath more than you might think. Empaths owe it to themselves to have a happily ever after. Remember that empaths attract narcissists; you must be on the lookout for them. Keep your energy and vibration high no matter what. A narcissist doesn't want to be fixed, no matter how much they pretend they need an empath's help. They will pretend they need you, all the while sucking your energy. Little by little, without even realizing it, an empath will begin to lose pieces of themselves.

Narcissists pull empaths away from their path or convince them that they are less than they are. Empaths know better, but deep down, they often don't believe they deserve better. This is how many empaths end up in toxic relationships with narcissists. Empaths are beautiful and strong, and empaths can overcome whatever they are facing today, tomorrow, and beyond.

When life throws a curveball, whether it's a bad breakup or being let go, many of us lower our vibration. These low vibrations drag us into what I call the dump. We wander around looking at other people's treasures and stop believing in ourselves. And if we stay in the dump, we start dumpster diving instead of looking for a way out. Then, when we start a new relationship or a new job, it's just like the one that sent us to the dump in the first place. And we wonder what's wrong with us as we continue to dig ourselves deeper into the muck.

When someone you love hurts you, it is a natural reaction to want to shield yourself and protect your heart to keep pain from entering. But a shut-down heart makes it impossible to allow in happiness, great opportunities, and good people. When you open your heart, you have room for growth, forgiveness, and change. Most of all, you can let love in again.

DON'T DRINK THE POISON

We've all had (or still have) a poisonous person in our lives. Poisonous people leave us feeling self-conscious, sad, depleted, and frustrated. They promise they will love us, but first we must become someone other than ourselves.

"You're way too sensitive," the man I loved told me. "If you were only stronger. If you had thicker skin. If you were…"

"Someone other than me," I replied with tears rolling down my cheeks. The same tears that angered him. The same tears that made him think I was weak. The truth was, I felt everything. I still do! I feel lies. I feel broken promises. I feel the hurt. I feel the grief. I always have. It wasn't until I learned how to create boundaries and stop trying to meet others' expectations that I realized that what some think of as weakness is actually strength. It takes a lot of strength for someone to feel everything and to not disappear in the hurt of it all.

I wasn't flawed, I am an empath. I used to call it a curse, but now I feel it's a blessing. Being an empath is just another part of who I am, and who you might be too. It's sort of like your eye color. You can get colored contacts to make your brown eyes blue, but they are still brown. You can pretend you aren't being hurt, but your empath heart and your soul know the truth.

The thing is that an empath has a certain light to them that makes them susceptible to those who want to steal that light, or snuff that light out because it makes them look bad. You don't have to feel guilty for releasing the toxic people in your life, no matter their relationship to you. You don't have to make room for those who continue to bring you pain. You don't have to heal everyone just because you are a healer. You don't have to sacrifice yourself by crossing oceans for those who wouldn't even jump a puddle for you.

You don't have to keep breaking your own heart by allowing others to control it. Cutting contact with toxic people will transform your life. That freedom allows you to thrive and leaves room for healthier relationships. Instead of absorbing toxic energy, forgiving, making excuses, and feeling everything, you attract higher-energy experiences and people. You deserve that. So do I.

Poisonous people are part of your family, your friendship circle, your church, your workplace, and maybe even your partner. Sometimes an empath is so used to drinking the same poison that we don't even recognize we are doing it.

HOW TO SPOT A POISONOUS PERSON

- **They are jealous.** Poisonous people are jealous of your success. They are happy when you fall flat on your face, and they don't help pick you up.

- **They are unreliable.** They make promises to you that they rarely keep.

- **They are constantly complaining.** No matter what they are doing, poisonous people find a reason to complain. They focus on the black cloud rather than the rainbow.

- **It's all about them.** Whatever is happening in their life is far more important than what is happening in your life. They can't relate that another has experienced anything closely related.

- **They make you feel guilty.** Poisonous people often use reverse psychology, making you feel as if you are the one who doesn't do enough and is the bad apple in the relationship. A healthy relationship won't ask you to sacrifice who you are or make you doubt yourself.

- **They pretend to be ambitious.** You will often hear a poisonous person talk about wanting to do this or that, yet the wanting and wishing typically don't come to fruition. If you call them out on it, they have plenty of excuses as to why something didn't work out.

- **They drain you.** Being around a poisonous person can drain you of your energy and physically make you sick.

HOW TO DETOX YOURSELF FROM A POISONOUS PERSON

- **Speak up.** This may not go well, but if it feels like there are more withdrawals in your relationship than deposits, it might be time to speak up about it. Speak your truth in a gentle and loving way. Offer suggestions for how the relationship could be better fostered for both of you. Expect feelings of guilt and anger to pop up during the discussion.

- **Set boundaries.** If you don't set boundaries, you allow the poison to keep infiltrating into your psyche. By enforcing your boundaries, whether physical or emotional, you are clearing your mind and detoxing to see if the person is worthy of staying in your circle.

- **Walk away.** Saying goodbye is painful, but poisonous people block your happiness and weaken your spirit. Love yourself enough to create a more peaceful environment around you and within you. By eliminating that which you cannot change, change what you can.

You cannot save someone; you can only love them.
And you can continue to do that by walking away.

Trauma Bonds

An empath feels everything, said and unsaid. And an empath falls in love with souls, not faces. An empath loves because they cannot help but love. When an empath walks away from a relationship, it's not because they are weak—it's because they are brave.

Being an empath has jaded many from time to time, but it rarely sticks. But it does no good to feel sorry for the choices made. Staring in the rearview mirror certainly does not get you to the next location. But I understand that it's not easy to move forward, especially when empaths have an innate ability to attract toxic people, energy vampires, narcissists, and gaslighters that use and abuse. And they come in all sizes, genders, and relationship statuses.

I had a close friend years ago. We found one another through our love of music, writing, and poetry, and we bonded over the shared grief of our pasts. It ended up being a beautiful friendship, but it was unhealthily wrapped in a toxic love. When she complained, I complained. When I complained, she complained. She relived her unsolved goals and lost loves, and it made me do the same. We jumped on the toxic train and sat there, complaining about the view the whole time.

One day she stopped calling. She didn't answer texts from me. There was no fight (that I knew of). No disagreement (that I realized). I went back over our text messages and emails. I replayed our phone calls in my head. And I mourned the loss of this friendship that had no closure.

Whether it is a romantic relationship or a friendship, the Universe hears conversations you don't, and sometimes it ends these toxic relationships because you won't. It doesn't mean that person is a bad person or that you are a bad person. It just means they are not a person you should have in your life. And even though it is in your best interest, it hurts, for sure. An empath is loyal for life, even when a relationship is toxic and you can't see it in the moment.

Spend that time considering the people in your circle. Do you perhaps need to detach rather than feed into the attachment? Do you have an unhealthy trauma bond? If you decide to end a toxic relationship, you don't need to be sorry for loving them, and you should never be sorry for walking away.

NOT EVERYONE WANTS TO BE HEALED

An empath is an expert at trauma bonding, which is when you become attached to a toxic person and are willing to accept less to stay in the misaligned relationship. Trauma bonding is similar to Stockholm syndrome, when a victim bonds with their abuser and sympathizes with them. An empath might believe they have found their perfect match, but instead, it's a trauma bond.

Abusers will depict themselves as needing to be healed and the healer takes the bait, like the fly to the spider. But they don't actually want to be healed; this is just a false pretense to attract an empath. This kind of relationship is never healthy, no matter what you want to believe. When someone shows you who they are, believe them the first time. The Universe is always showing you truths; don't place doubt on your gift of intuition.

There comes a time when you have to step away from a trauma bond. It may feel as if you walked through a burning forest, because emotionally you did. You may feel like you fell down a hundred times, but it's that one time you get up and keep going that counts.

You likely weren't their first victim. You won't be the last. But you are a survivor, dear empath.

THE BROKEN

Sometime the person you love the most is the person you can trust the least. An empath gives second, third, and fourth chances—sometimes they give hundreds. They throw their love at people like confetti, and then they wonder why they feel so empty when they are the only one picking up all the jagged pieces of the relationship.

Empaths see the good in the broken. They see who someone can be rather than who they are in the moment. Plus, the broken don't always show their fractures all at once. An empath is okay to grow together as the relationship progresses because they know that everyone is unfinished. An empath will take the lows and let their partner take the highs, but do you see how imbalanced that truly is? A healthy partner won't let this happen, but not everyone understands an empath's heart.

An empath sees a person's true self on a soul level, but that doesn't mean the person wants to grow into who they could be. There are the broken who know they are broken and are willing to work on themselves, and there are the broken who do not care if they cut someone else with their brokenness. This doesn't mean the broken are necessarily off limits to empaths, because we are all broken to some degree, but if a relationship is damaging you, then you have to prioritize your self-preservation. There's a saying that whatever you are not changing, you are choosing. It's a small but powerful checklist. What are you changing in your life to help yourself?

Think about a relationship like a train. There are many trains available to us, but most empaths decide to take the broken-down train. The sign hangs by one bolt. The seats don't have any cushion. Springs pop up, making every bump hurt. The ride is extra noisy. There's no heating when it's cold or air-conditioning when it's hot. The people on the train all smell, and nobody uses their headphones. Instead, they talk loudly on speakerphone or listen to music and videos on full blast. Now, you could've walked just a bit more to get on a better train. Instead, you chose to get on the broken-down train.

"When will I find my person, Kristy?" is something I'm asked every single day by someone. The truth is, I can't predict when, but I can make you realize that it's time to get on another train. An empath will come up with a million excuses for not changing course, hoping whatever they are doing will be enough. It won't. They will get on the same broken-down train, with the torn seats and the smelly people, hoping someone new will show up on that train. Oh, there will be new people who show up on that train—but they aren't yours, because you don't belong on that train. You deserve to be on the shiny new train.

If you don't shift and grow, you will continue to meet the broken and hope it will be different the next time. It won't. You will allow yourself to be heartbroken. You will keep forgiving. You will allow the toxic silent treatments, believing that if you change—if you are better at sex, better at cooking, better at asking permission, better at whatever else—then you will keep your partner. But you shouldn't be keeping a broken partner because you deserve a person who loves you the same way you love them, and you don't need to change anything about yourself.

I once dated a guy who told me he'd love me more if I was a brunette, so I dyed my hair. *I dyed my hair!* His response when he saw me was, "Well, that's a start." I stayed with him for a couple months until I came to realize I needed to change trains. Fast.

The next train wasn't any better, honestly, but I continued to switch trains until I felt comfortable with who I was no matter who joined me on the journey. I was okay if it was just me. It was then that I met my now-husband.

SECOND-GUESSING

Many empaths second-guess themselves. They second-guess their feelings, perceptions, and memories. Empaths are super intuitive and often trust the advice they give others, but when it comes to themselves, they have their own doubts. Like I did—I thought, *Maybe I* would *be better looking as a brunette.* No! *What?* No! Feeling minimized by someone else isn't love. It's crushing. It's smothering. It's suffocating. It's crazy, and it makes an empath feel crazy. Add in an energy vampire, narcissist, and/or gaslighter who plays on an empath's doubts, and the combination can be debilitating and depressive. But an empath is often convinced it's better to feel pain than nothing at all. Some empaths turn to addictions to mask their hurt or guilt after sharing their soul with someone they intuitively knew they shouldn't have.

ENERGY VAMPIRES, NARCISSISTS, AND GASLIGHTERS, OH MY!

Energy vampires don't have fangs and they don't drink blood, but they are just as scary. An energy vampire is someone whose energy and life force are weak from stress or trauma, so they unconsciously (and sometimes consciously) drain the energy from those around them in order to feel better, hurting their victims in the process. Energy vampires could be your mom, your dad, your sibling, your best friend, your spouse, your child, your boss—pretty much anybody. It could even be you.

Narcissists and gaslighters are the broken who convince you that is *you* who is broken. Many times, the victims of narcissists are those in the healing fields. Most are empaths because they are open and willing to help others, and therefore they can be manipulated by the masters of manipulation.

Yes, empaths are called to the most broken people in the world, but you do not have to answer that call. You are not a failure for letting go of the need to save everyone.

COMMON BEHAVIORS OF ENERGY VAMPIRES, NARCISSISTS, AND GASLIGHTERS

- They feed off any attention.
- They say that they want to get better and be a better person, yet they make no effort to grow and instead make excuses as to why they can't grow.
- They are seldom happy, no matter what.
- They discredit you by making other people think that you're crazy, irrational, or unstable.
- They wear a mask of confidence, assertiveness, and/or fake compassion.
- They make you doubt yourself.
- They change the subject when you bring up something you want to talk about or are concerned with.
- They discount you, often making statements like "You didn't remember that right," "You're always exaggerating," and "You are always so dramatic."
- They minimize you by accusing you of being too sensitive.

- They continue to minimize you when you get upset by saying, "I was just joking. You are always so serious."
- They refuse to acknowledge your feelings and thoughts.
- They like to pick fights and force others around them to choose sides.
- They often want advice and/or money.
- They want constant compassion, but they don't reciprocate it.
- When you try and separate yourself, they try to retaliate.
- You may feel depressed, fearful, angry, sad, and unhappy when they are around, which causes you to start arguments that have no rhyme or reason.
- Attention—both good and bad—equates to energy, and this is what they feed off, so their moods tend to swing like a pendulum.

HOW TO PROTECT YOURSELF

- Avoid any interaction with people who have been known to drain, depress, or irritate you when you are feeling ill, weak, tired, or stressed.
- Surround yourself with positive people until your energy is strong again, or else you will continue to be drained of your lifeblood.
- Seek out a therapist.
- Seek out a trusted friend.

An empath often has their guard down, thinking this is their gift (or curse), but it's a falsehood. An empath is a better healer when they are better protected and more balanced. Every empath needs a healthy support system.

CODE BLUE

If you're an empath or a highly sensitive person, you've probably developed a destructive habit over the years of trying to educate toxic people to be more empathic or considerate of who you are. You've learned how to forgive no matter how much pain you were in, which invalidates your own feelings.

When an empath works on building healthy boundaries, you slowly realize it is not your job or responsibility to fix anyone. You begin sensing the code blues. (In the medical field, the term *code blue* is universally recognized as an emergency.) For an empath, there will always be code blues, but you aren't always on duty.

As I finish writing this book, I'm sitting in a hospital room watching my husband fight multiple myeloma, plasma cancer. I used to pray nobody in my family got cancer because with cancer treatments, I feel all the empathetic traits: I feel ill; I feel every cancer cell in my own body; I feel every chemotherapy treatment; I feel the exhaustion. When I read for someone with cancer, I had to excuse myself to the bathroom so I could feel all the feelings. Then my husband was diagnosed. Chuck received high doses of chemotherapy, a stem cell transplant, and a nicked artery during a routine cardiac atrial procedure. All the while, there's a global pandemic, an uproarious election, and continued systemic racism. The techniques I've shared in this book are tried and true during some of the hardest times in my life. An empath doesn't need to sacrifice themselves during a time of suffering, even when that suffering is happening to one of your favorite people.

THE GRIEVING EMPATH

A grieving empath must be especially careful with depression and anxiety. They may look okay, but they are wearing the weight of everyone else's pain when nobody is watching. They are likely simply going through the motions, pretending, so that nobody feels the need to care for them. They are the one silently drowning. It's a heavy and complicated costume that the empath wears, feeling pulled down by everything. Death changes an empath, but it can help them grow. It doesn't necessarily have to be a negative change.

Terri's husband Drew was diagnosed with prostate cancer. He came home one day and just dropped the news at the dinner table with a bag of McDonalds burgers.

"We will fight this," Terri told Drew. "We will do everything to keep you alive."

Drew didn't contest, and during the next few months he continued to go about his life as if there was nothing wrong. He went to work, he took the family on vacation, and he visited the doctor for his weekly chemotherapy.

"He never once complained," Terri told me. "Even when I could tell he was tired, he would still mow the lawn, and he carpooled the kids to and from school."

Ten months after his diagnosis, Drew started to become increasingly ill until he was lying on the couch, looking grey and thinner than his family had ever seen him. He was dying.

"We will get another opinion, Drew," Terri cried. "I will call around on Monday."

Unfortunately, Monday didn't come for Drew. He passed away that Sunday, surrounded by his family.

"He went to work on Friday and was gone by Monday. I was so confused about how it progressed so fast," Terri told me. "I felt terrible, as if I let him down. Then I was cleaning his home office." When Terri cleaned out her husband's desk, right in the center drawer was a letter from Drew's oncologist that spelled out his diagnosis. His cancer was terminal, and it was estimated he had only had twelve months to live.

"He never mentioned the letter. He never told me the diagnosis was terminal. I don't know if he was in denial or if he just wanted to keep hope alive. I don't know if he didn't want us to know there was an expiration date—if that might've meant the days would be filled with more tears than there were. I don't know, but I feel terrible that he felt he couldn't tell me. I just feel terrible," Terri said, putting her head in her hands.

Then she wiped her tears away, looked at me, and laughed. "You know what else I feel terrible about? The day before he died, I was mad at him. He had this annoying habit of humming when he ate. It drove me batty. I had to turn on the television or radio to tune him out. Now, I'd give anything to hear him annoy me with his loud eating." She then tried to imitate Drew's chewing and humming, and we laughed until we cried.

"And…He ruined McDonalds for me too!"

We laughed again.

Death is always hard, whether you are an empath or not. Terri was an empath. She was a fixer. She felt guilty for things that weren't hers to carry. And when empaths are knee-deep in grief, they second-guess everything. They often want to disappear rather than feel another feeling because they are already overwhelmed with all the feelings. Being able to find laughter is crucial for an empath to heal.

COMPASSION FATIGUE

The end of each year often pushes many of us to reflect. We contemplate the losses, forgetting about the wins. We tabulate the worst moments of the year, often not remembering the wonderful things that happened. With that unbalanced energy comes sadness and depression.

I've caught myself saying, "I hope next year is better than this year" and "I'm so done with this year," more so during 2020 than any other. But why? I mean, I have my list of losses that I could bore you with, but I have my list of gains too, and they sit there quietly wondering why they don't get the same fanfare. This soul-aching energy loop of burnout is called *compassion fatigue*.

An empath feels other people's feelings, and a compassionate empath takes that to the next level by trying to solve other people's problems. But compassionate empaths have to remember that we each carry our own backpack. In that backpack is our love, our hurt, our losses, and our gains. It's all the experiences, memories, and lessons that we've had in this lifetime. It's the time your brother threw a football at your face and did more than give you a bloody nose, he made you wary of trusting him. It's your first crush and the first time you felt crushed. It's the time your mom didn't go to your choir concert for whatever reason. It's the hurt when your grandparent passed away but nobody in the family helped teach you how to grieve, instead deciding that his name couldn't be uttered again. It's your first job and your first job loss. It's the time your child told you they didn't love you, even though they really didn't mean it, but it hurt anyway. It's all the times you made exceptions and excuses, when you forgave and said it was no problem, but really it did matter. Whatever it was, however small it was, it's all of that. And you carry it every day. Empaths carry their backpack, not allowing anyone else to help them along their journey, and not only are they carrying their load, but then they start carrying someone else's heavy backpack.

And another.

And another.

And another.

When the empath finally falls under the crushed weight, those who've handed over their loads look on and call out, "Why are you so weak?" "Maybe you need therapy!" "Why are you so depressed?" "Why are you so angry?" "I've got the same problems and I'm doing fine. Just get up." They forget the fact that they feel okay because you've been carrying their backpacks the entire time. And all the while, they keep sneaking more and more weight into their backpack when they think you aren't looking.

Compassion fatigue is real. It happens to those in the medical profession. It happens to therapists, ministers, moms and dads, and healers too. It happens to those empaths who are so busy helping and fixing others that they forget to take time to empty their backpacks out. Self-care is imperative for everyone, especially for an empath.

WAYS FOR EMPATHS TO PRACTICE SELF-CARE

We all know about basic self-care, but the healers and helpers of the world feel bad doing it because taking time for themselves feels wrong. Often, we do things for others not because we expect anything, but because it's who we are. It comes with a price, though, and it's so important to take a step back and take care of you so that the price isn't compassion fatigue, anger, illness, or bitterness. So:

- See a therapist if you want.
- Set boundaries. (This is so hard for a helper, but you must.)
- Practice positive self-talk. (It's easy for empaths to be nice to others, but are you being nice to yourself?)
- Socialize with friends.
- Journal. Vent your emotions.
- Meditate and be mindful.
- Release the need to save everyone.
- Empty out your backpack regularly.
- Say no to people who try to hand you their backpack or sneak their issues into your backpack.

Unchain Yourself

If you're feeling like you are chained by life's circumstances and are spending too much time dumpster diving, try this quick meditation.

1. Close your eyes and envision heavy chains wrapped around you.
2. See your guide or angel step forward with just one key. Your guide/angel unlocks the lock and slowly, the chains begin to drop.
3. With each chain you shrug off, the more you feel like yourself and the less you are tied down.

EMOTIONAL HOARDING

Have you ever been passed over for a promotion and immediately began looking for another job? Or gotten out of a relationship and immediately rebounded? So often we try to keep up with the Joneses by comparing our life with someone else's before we've even dealt with the emotional clutter. It might not be obvious that you're dragging that emotional clutter behind you when you show up at a job interview for a position you don't really want, but your pride is hurt. And you probably don't share that emotional mess on the date you really don't want to be on, but you would much rather be watching a tearjerker movie and eating a gallon of ice cream. Sure, there are times when you must deal with something and move on, but make sure you don't just ditch your emotional mess in the closet and pretend it's not really there, because eventually it will come find you—and it might be harder to deal with in the future.

An emotional empath tends to emotionally hoard because they are afraid to ask for help or bother someone else with their problems. They often keep spiritual cords attached to them from their relationships, whether the cord is current or in the past. And the more cords, the heavier the spirit.

Celestine came to me with a laundry list of issues and felt horrible about it. Her energy was low, and she was struggling with her job and her relationships.

"The guy I'm dating told me I was too intense and always busy, and he couldn't deal with my swinging moods, which honestly are probably caused by my constantly busy schedule that makes me intense." She started laughing. "I have to laugh because I've cried so much over this."

"I think it's time to do a cleanup. Stick with me." I stopped her from making a defensive response. "You know all that clutter you think you might really need? Either use it or toss it, but stop storing it."

Celestine nodded to show that she understood.

"You can't grow a beautiful and healthy garden when you didn't take the time to clean up the weeds. To you, every weed is special, but it's not serving you well."

Whether you are (im)patiently awaiting the love of your life, your dream home, a baby, a new job, or fill in the blank, you have to squash the panic and worry. Instead, think about what you want, not what you'll just accept.

DUCK DUCK

Hayden and Pippa were a young couple who came to see me for a session. The session was a Christmas gift from Pippa's sister. Immediately, I felt the tension between them. Pippa's arms were crossed, wrapped tightly around her chest. Hayden and Pippa sat on the same couch next to one another, but they sat several inches away one another, not one part of their bodies touching. It didn't take an intuitive to see they were squabbling. But they both were pretending to be fine, at least for my sake.

"Well," I started hesitantly, "Your guides think you two are perfect for one another, but obviously there's some understanding that needs to happen to balance and secure the relationship."

Hayden stared at me while Pippa bit her bottom lip, both staying silent in response.

Hayden took a breath in. "She's so emotional. No matter what I do or say, she takes offense, and apparently I don't do or say anything right!"

I said, "Arguments happen. Disagreements are normal, and I'm not Doctor Phil or a licensed therapist, but I have had many relationships of my own, and I can tell you that sometimes emotions can run high. Some people find it's healthy to back off for a bit instead of taking passive-aggressive jabs or offering a yucky dish of cold treatments."

A grandmother energy came through right then and stood next to Hayden. She pointed at her wedding ring and then back to him. "He's waiting for perfect, and nothing will be perfect," she tsked. "He's setting himself up to lose her."

I sighed hard before sharing the message.

"I can't help that I'm careful." Hayden matched my hard sigh. "She's in debt. I don't want her debt. She thinks she can start her own business, yet she's in debt, so what about that says she can be successful?"

"When someone doesn't believe in us, we often stop believing in ourselves too," I said, softening my tone.

Pippa had been patiently listening, but I could see her mind spinning with a spiral of responses. I asked her to take a deep breath and tell us what she was feeling.

"I'm trying to make things better. Why am I the only one who works at understanding you and your flaws—because we know you have flaws too—but you can't seem to understand me?" Pippa wiped away her tears.

"She allows her emotions to run out of control *all the time*," Hayden said to me. "She needs to get her ducks in a row, but she likes her ducks running all over the place, despite my attempts to help," Hayden defensively snapped.

Pippa's brow furrowed. She briefly turned to study Hayden's face before standing up and walking to my office door. "I have to go check on my ducks," she growled before she left.

"See?" Hayden pointed. "How can I help her if she won't let me help her? She wants to go to counseling, but I don't need counseling, I need her to do what I tell her to do."

Ouch.

Pippa and Hayden had been together for three years, and Hayden had been constantly reminding Pippa of her weaknesses in the hopes that it would inspire her to do better. But nobody likes to be criticized, and it's hurtful for anyone to be told they have stupid ideas. It's hurtful when someone says you are overreacting or makes you feel ignored or excluded. Pippa was an empath, and like most empaths, she had given up pieces of her own life so that Hayden could succeed. When Pippa decided to do something for herself, Hayden felt excluded and Pippa felt confused. The empath in her wanted to balance this, but she was afraid if she walked her own path, she'd lose Hayden. But the more she didn't walk her path, the more she lost herself.

I said, "Maybe she doesn't want you to problem-solve her, but to listen to her. She's smart, Hayden. She's emotional, but emotional isn't a negative. Emotional can be passionate. But you must love her good passion just the same as you must tolerate and learn how to deal with her sassy passion. If you genuinely love her."

Hayden stared at his hands.

"You don't want to go to counseling, and yet you are so busy counseling her that you aren't listening to her. Pippa is the one for you—at least that's what your grandma says, and grandma's ring is available for the proposal—but there are some compromises you have to make. And she has to too."

"I don't like anyone telling me what to do, so why would I expect her to?" Hayden said thoughtfully. Then he gave another sigh that seemed to release years of tension. "Now what do I do?"

I pointed to the door and smiled. "You know."

A year later I received a wedding invitation in the mail, along with a small rubber duck and a note that read, "We're still learning when to let the ducks run around free-range and when to put them to bed. It's a work in progress, but we're doing it together."

YOU REALLY GET ME

Someone who doesn't understand an empath can be quick to judge them with words such as crazy, emotional, messy, sensitive, oversensitive, negative, damaged, naïve, and so on. Don't take reactions at face value, though, because while an empath may be demonstrating their sensitivity, there's more going on behind the scenes.

For example, an empath may have just gone to a supermarket and felt overwhelmed by the fluorescent lights and the noise of the shoppers. If you then decided to ask them a complicated question like "What are we doing for dinner?" it wouldn't go over well because the empath is in the middle of an empath storm, which can be painful and confusing for anyone. You would never ask someone trying to get away from a tornado, "What are we doing for dinner?" It's the same thing. Sounds crazy, but it's far from it.

Once you recognize the empaths in your life, you can better handle their storms by:

- **Being curious.** Ask questions about their experiences.

- **Listening.** Often an empath just wants to be heard, even if you don't understand what they are going through.

- **Trying not to fix things.** When an empath opens up and you immediately try to fix things, you challenge the reason for their emotions. You might think problem-solving is helpful but instead, be curious and listen. If the empath asks for your help, go ahead! But instantly trying to fix things can make an empath feel unheard.

PERMISSION GRANTED

Empaths are kindhearted, sometimes to a fault, and will put other's needs before their own. This becomes habitual, but it's also emotionally destructive. If an empath is in a relationship with a narcissist, the narcissist will take advantage of this trait and control everything from sex and finances to the remote controller. Narcissists are award-winning actors and will emotionally damage an empath until they become a mere shadow of themselves. Awareness and education are the best defense for an empath; this helps them see that they need care and love too.

"I'm gonna take a shower, okay?" I asked my husband.

"Sure," he answered, munching on a handful of potato chips, not taking his eyes off one of his favorite football teams, the New Orleans Saints. (Our hometown team is the Detroit Lions, but we need a winning team to root for too.)

Showers are my escape and have been since I was a kid. I love taking a hot shower with my radio blasting or a positive podcast playing while I daydream. It's honestly my favorite place to get my creative juices stirring. But on this day, I was in a mood, and my question to my husband irritated me. Why had I asked him if I could take a shower? I paid the mortgage too. Heck, I was the only one who cleaned the shower and refilled the soap! So why was I asking for his permission?

When I talked about this with a friend, she said, "I ask my husband if I can take a shower, if I can have a glass of water, if I can go to Target, and pretty much everything."

"Do you have to ask him, or are you doing it to be nice?" I asked. "Because I think if I told Chuck I was going to run to Alaska and I'd be back in a week, he'd say 'Sure.'" I laughed because I realized that whenever I asked Chuck a question, he usually wasn't even listening to what I was saying. I was asking for permission for something so ridiculous; I wasn't buying a new car with our money—I was showering *my* body.

My friend's answer was surprising, though.

"Oh, I need to ask," she said. "He'd be mad if I didn't."

I didn't respond because I was shocked. *Was this 1790? Did we turn the clocks back centuries during the last daylight saving time instead of an hour?* When my husband and I went through our traditional wedding vows, I told him I wasn't fan of the "obey your spouse" part. I will love you. I will honor you. But I'm not a golden retriever, and neither is he. We are partners, so "obey" felt too controlling, especially after all the controlling and toxic relationships we had had.

An empath often feels the need to ask for permission, though. Now, there's a difference between doing it out of courtesy and actually asking for permission. I wasn't one to judge my friend's relationship, but I wasn't about to ask Chuck for permission again.

"I'm taking a shower," I told my husband the next day.

"Okay," he replied.

No permission needed.

FLIP IT

I've taught many empaths that when they feel unworthy or devalued, they can use it as a learning experience instead of sitting in sadness. I teach this technique to both adults and children. Grab a sheet of paper and divide it into two columns. In the left column, write out how you feel or what others have said to you. In the right column, flip the negative into a positive. For example:

That	This
"You are so sensitive."	I'm so glad that I'm sensitive because I can help others.
"You are so clingy."	I am going to work on being more independent.
"You are so intense."	I am going to try new ways to relax.

HELP, DON'T HURT AN EMPATH

Those who aren't an empath (or maybe just aren't as sensitive) often feel as if they are helping with their words. Instead, their words can sometimes be seen as insensitive and cause further relationship issues. Here are some examples of things you shouldn't say to an empath, and what you could say instead.

What Not to Say or Do	Why Not?	What to Say or Do Instead
"You are so sensitive."	This is an empath trait. It is their superpower.	"I know you feel everything. Is there anything I can do to help?"
"Are you crying again?"	Yep, an empath will cry, but asking if they are crying again will only make them feel unheard, and this will make them cry more.	"Cry it out. Do you want to be held?"

What Not to Say or Do	Why Not?	What to Say or Do Instead
"You are always tired."	An empath can get tired easily. Feeling and sensing everything can be exhausting.	"It must be exhausting feeling and sensing everything. Why don't you take a quick nap or do a meditation?"
"Stop taking things so personally."	To an empath, everything is personal, and you saying that is a slap in the face.	"Are you feeling overwhelmed right now? Is there anything I can do to help you?"
"It was just a joke."	Empaths can take a joke, but when the joke is hurtful or sarcastic and then protected by the phrase "It's just a joke," it discounts their reaction.	"I wasn't thinking. I'm sorry."
"I've been through worse."	Small things can feel huge to an empath, and life situations aren't a competition.	"I'm sorry about what you are going through. Do you want to talk about it?"
"You need to calm down."	I'm pretty sure nobody has ever calmed down after being told to calm down.	"Do you want to go for a walk? We don't even have to talk unless you want to."
"I know how you are feeling."	You might have an idea of what an empath is feeling, but there's often no true solidarity in the statement.	"Do you want to tell me how you are feeling, and do you want my advice?"

What Not to Say or Do	Why Not?	What to Say or Do Instead
"Look on the bright side."	An empath knows both sides of a situation, so if they aren't seeing the bright side, they are viewing the dark side.	Instead of telling an empath to look on the bright side, help them see the bright side by playing upbeat music, watching a comedy with them, or taking them out for dinner.

FINDING HEALTHY LOVE

An empath naturally has a soft heart and a romantic soul. Most single empaths long for their soul mate, but they feel smothered in relationships and might hightail it out of there—unless it's the right person.

If you are being loved by an empath, consider yourself blessed. Empaths are natural givers; whether they are giving their time, their love, or their money, everything is given selflessly. All empaths want to do is make everyone happy.

But empaths need to remember that they cannot fix everyone, if anyone. Empaths cannot always be the hero. Some people create their own storms and then get mad when it rains. Parasitic people will take and take until empaths have nothing to give them, and then they move on. Letting go of what is unhealthy doesn't make you a bad person—it means you are finally realizing that you deserve a happy and healthy life. There are lots of ways an empath can attract healthy love into their life.

SURROUND YOURSELF WITH POSITIVE PEOPLE

Stop hanging out with negative people who don't support your dreams and aspirations and only feed into your stress and worry. This also goes for those you encounter online, especially on social media accounts like Twitter and Facebook. You have every right to create boundaries by blocking someone or hitting the unfriend button.

CHOOSE WHAT SPEAKS TO YOU

If you are wondering if someone in your life is legit, you already know the answer. Choose the people and the situations that speak to what you want in your life. Spell out what you want in your life and don't take second best, but be realistic. If you want that promotion and someone else got it, don't fester, pout, and cry. Instead, keep your focus on what you want to happen. Then a better position might fall into your lap.

STOP ASKING PERMISSION

It is sad to say this, but so many people are afraid of their friends/family/coworkers becoming more successful than they are. If you are asking for permission to follow your dream or to go after something, more times than not, someone is going to find fault with it. This is only going to make you second-guess yourself. Stop asking permission and follow your heart. Choose what speaks to you!

STOP FEELING GUILTY FOR YOUR SUCCESSES

You deserve to be happy. Yes, you! You are entitled to celebrate your successes and you deserve to love your life. Just because your best friend or relative is going through something doesn't mean you have to negate what is going right in your life. You can actually help them out by being successful and happy. Oh, they may hate you for a moment, but happiness is just as contagious as depression.

CONFRONT YOUR FEARS HEAD-ON

Sometimes we know what we don't want more than we know what we *do* want. When you allow fear to be your best friend, you lose your identity. Make a list of what you are afraid of. Confront those fears head-on by naming them and looking at them realistically. If they are fears that you have no control over (which tends to be most of them), then simply replace that fear with what you want to happen. For example, let's say you are afraid of losing your job. You don't control that, your boss does, so spend your time doing the best job you possibly can instead of worrying about losing your job. If you are worrying over never finding someone that will love you, spend that time loving yourself instead.

IT'S NOT YOU, IT'S ME

Empaths often don't believe they are good enough, yet they become frustrated when they don't receive their fair share in life. Fear of rejection and chronic anxiety trick and manipulate an empath's spirit into a false inner dialogue of not being deserving of good things in life. This stifles their intuition and kicks the mind into overdrive as they imagine worst-case scenarios. Some empaths get bitter. Some push. Some run. And some discover (or rediscover) their inner power and realize that love is the highest vibration of all.

Years ago, I had just gone through *another* bad breakup. Remember, empaths put their all into their love life; they fall hard, even when they know they're not falling for the right person. At the time, I didn't understand that the Universe was removing negative people from my life.

It wasn't long after the breakup that I was set up on a date. It was a Sunday afternoon, and we were going to meet for lunch at a local restaurant. When we got to the restaurant, I looked at him and realized he wasn't at all my type, and by the way he was looking at me, I could tell I wasn't his type either. We sat down and I ordered a salad. He ordered a cheeseburger and fries.

"What do you do for a living?" he asked me.

Instead of telling him my corporate title, I spit out that I was a spiritual medium. It was the first time I'd ever said that out loud, and I had no idea how or why I would even say something like that. As if on cue, our food was delivered right then. Instead of reacting to the whole "I see dead people" thing, he replied, "That's so cool, but can you pass the ketchup?" That's when I knew I was in trouble. Maybe my type—which obviously had not gone well for me in the past—wasn't my type after all! Mind blown.

This man was living an hour away from me, but after work on Fridays, he would show up at my door and stay the whole weekend—until one Thursday night several months into our relationship, when I told him we needed to break up. I couldn't give him a reason; no, I hadn't met someone else. The truth was, I was falling for him, and I didn't want to get hurt again, especially so soon. I still had bruises I was healing. I needed space, I told him.

The next night I came home from work, fixed dinner for me and my kids, and settled in to watch *Gilmore Girls*. Then I heard a car door slam and a familiar knock. I walked to the door, and there he was. Standing there with takeout and his overnight bag. I opened the door, confused. He gave me a quick kiss on the lips and headed to the kitchen.

I stared at him for a bit, then said, "I told you that I needed space and we were broken up. Do you remember that conversation?"

He plated the food and set it on the dining room table. I mean, he didn't even notice that I had dinner on the stove. He didn't ask if I'd eaten. He just sat down at the table with his food and pointed to the plate he set in front of me. I didn't know whether to be mad, sad, or what. So I just stood there, arms crossed and confused. After a few bites, he set down his fork and looked at me.

"I heard the conversation, but I didn't believe the words you used in the conversation. You're just scared. I get it. But there's nothing to be afraid of. So, you go watch your show and I'll do the dishes."

Unbelievably, I ended up marrying him. The reason my relationship with Chuck works is because he is also an empath. He understands my sensitivity at a soul level. Although his empath traits are different, we feel like we were spiritually created in the same crayon box. That doesn't mean my sensitivity doesn't sometimes bother him (it does) or that his sensitivity doesn't bug me once in a while (it does), but the better we understand ourselves, the better we understand one another and our relationship.

THE BEST PARTNERS FOR AN EMPATH ARE…

- **Another Empath:** While this sounds like a great idea—and it can be, as they understand your idiosyncrasies—it's intense. If you enter a relationship with another empath, emotions and boundaries must be clear and communicated.

- **A Strong Person:** Empaths can be a handful, and they need someone emotionally strong who can handle their ebbs and flows.

- **An Intelligent Person:** Just because an empath is emotional doesn't mean they aren't smart. Most empaths are super smart, which is why they get so frustrated about their sensitive ways. Empaths need an intelligent partner who can understand where they are coming from.

- **A Good Listener:** An empath needs someone to talk to and to bounce ideas off. They need someone who will listen instead of just trying to problem-solve or fix the situation for them.

COMPROMISE AND CONCERTS

Empaths often avoid doing things that make them feel uncomfortable. As much as it is good to know thyself, empaths can get stuck in their comfort zone, but love often pushes the boundaries. Worst-case scenario, an empath might want to make their partner happy so badly that they sacrifice their own peace of mind and energy. Best-case scenario, the empath might grow through the experience and discover that they like something new.

I have always loved the theater. I loved seeing Broadway shows. I loved participating in community theater. I loved blasting soundtracks and belting out show tunes. My ex hated it, so I quit doing all of it. Instead, I spent my time watching him play video games. An unfair trade if you ask me, but I was in love. (Eye roll.)

After the breakup, I was determined not to give up things I loved, no matter what. When I met my husband, I was participating in a community theater show. Chuck hated it, but he never once asked me to quit. Instead, he went to every one of my plays. Sure, there were times he fell asleep in the audience, but he went. He has bought me tickets to *Wicked*, and he simply goes into another room when I watch *The Sound of Music* for the hundredth time. I'd do the same thing for him, even if it makes me uncomfortable sometimes. It's called compromise.

In order to keep our relationship balanced, Chuck and I make healthy sacrifices. I will say, though, that thanks to compromise, I've ended up loving some things I thought I would hate. Including live music, despite the many obstacles I seem to attract while there.

TRUST THE VIBE

Have you ever heard a song and it just made you angry? Or sad? Or happy? Empaths can feel the emotions of music running through their soul and spirit. Music raises our vibration. It helps us find, release, and express joy, sorrow, and pain that we might not have been able to convey. Music can even help us process a past situation that we'd simply stored away by tuning in to that vibration and helping us deal with it once and for all.

Music has always been my escape from the outside world. Ever since I was little, you could find me playing an instrument, singing, and/or dancing. I started singing in the choir when I was in kindergarten, and I did so until I graduated from high school. I began percussion lessons when I was in fourth grade, playing everything from Bon Jovi to Metallica to gospel music. My first concert was Adam Ant. It wasn't my type of music, but he was my best friend's favorite. It wasn't my scene; I dressed in long tunics, stirrup pants, lots of bracelets, and headbands. (Ironically, that is how I still dress today.) At the concert hall, most people were dressed in leather and had multiple piercings. When the music began, though, we all became one.

The energy at the Adam Ant concert was intense and exhilarating, but I knew live music wasn't my thing because of all the people.

Okay, maybe not *all* the people, but the *obnoxious* people: people who drink too much, who partake in drugs, and who overall have a great time. I'm not against having a great time, but for those of us who are sensitive to everything, the noise and energy of all those people is a lot.

My husband loves live music, and in every relationship there are compromises and sacrifices. So, I go and see live music, but I protect myself by carrying an abundance of crystals and magical potions with me. Before I go into the venue, I ask for an army of angels to surround me. I also look for several exit strategies when I'm at the venue, and when I come home, I have to shower off the energy, literally and figuratively.

When I am not vibrationally secure at a venue, I open myself up for all kinds of crazy. It's sort of like when you hold your purse or wallet close to your person; a thief who knows what they are doing can still bump into you and steal what they need. At a venue, I'll think I have everything tucked into place, but then I run into experienced energy stealers. Like the guy at the Alice Cooper concert who peed on my foot while drinking a beer and looked me straight in the eye. Now, this guy did offer me a swig of his beer as an apology. I thanked him kindly and ran off to the bathroom. A nightmare for an empath.

Or there was the girl at the John Waite concert who decided to pick a fight with me for no reason. Not just any old fight either— she tried to take a swing at me in the middle of Waite crooning "Missing You."

Or the guy at the Zac Brown concert who spilled his nachos all over my white sweater (yeah, I know, what was I thinking?!) and then pulled me into the aisle to dance with him. Nacho cheese was dripping off my left arm. My husband quickly grabbed me out of his grasp before any dancing ensued.

Oh, and there was middle-aged lady who called me all kinds of names at the U2 concert because I was sitting down for a minute on the stadium bench. I mean, I had just danced for an hour to Florence and the Machine and I was tired, plus I was overwhelmed by the amount of people that were packed into the stadium like sardines.

I once sat in the middle of a large row at a B. B. King concert and ended up holding a lady who was sobbing. I offered to drive a girl home after her boyfriend broke up with her right as OneRepublic took the stage, only for the couple to make up and then make out as Ryan Tedder sang "Apologize." I've been pushed, hit, yelled at, peed on, and more. The joke is that most of those concerts were tame! My friends and family members prefer to not sit by me at a concert because I'm an empath magnet.

A couple years back, Chuck, who is a faithful Alice Cooper and Cheap Trick fan, asked if I wanted to go see Billy Idol.

"The only thing is, Billy Idol is opening for—" he paused and then sneered "Bryan Adams!" in his best Billy Idol imitation that looked more like a bad Elvis.

I'd seen Billy before, in Vegas of all places. This was back in my wild and crazy years, which were dull by comparison. I'd never really had any interest in seeing Bryan, although I wasn't against it, so Chuck bought the tickets and I forgot all about it until a few nights beforehand.

"We'll just leave a couple songs into Bryan Adams, if that's what you want to do," I told Chuck. We always had to have an exit strategy. Actually, *I* always had to have an exit strategy. One of my empath anxieties was being stuck in the traffic jam trying to leave a venue. I sound like I'm 110 years old, I know.

The night of the concert, we got to the venue early and started to chat with the ushers. We were *that* early; we should've accepted jobs as volunteer ushers. I always get to a venue early so I can chameleon into the vibration. That year Chuck and I had already gotten rained out of several outdoor concerts, one that included tornadoes and torrential floods, so several of the ushers recognized us. We all laughed together, and Chuck and I hoped we weren't the bad luck charm. But it was a beautiful night, and Billy Idol came on stage with so much energy. He was entertaining from beginning to end.

"So, a couple songs in, yeah, and then we leave?" Chuck asked me in between sets.

"Sounds good," I replied, hugging him, but also looking around to see how we'd get out of the venue. The sun had set, and everything looks different in the moonlight.

Then Bryan came out. He looked sleek, his voice was strong, and he was humble and real. Even though there were 10,000 people there, the music transported me to a place of peacefulness. I don't know if the audience was struck silent by the music like I was or if I had been transported back in time by the soundtrack of my teenage years. Or both. Nothing phased me for the entire seventy-minute set.

Not only did Chuck and I stay until the end, but we also stayed until the house lights came on. I was crying. My contacts had hardened from the surrounding smoke and everything was blurry from my tears, so I couldn't see. I had to gather myself so I didn't trip over my own feet or someone else's. Oddly enough, a Rob Thomas (Matchbox Twenty) concert not long after had a similar effect on me. Was I using a better crystal or a more potent potion, or had my angels received a promotion of powers? Nope. I had just found my natural frequency, figuratively and literally, and I felt invincible!

The weeks after the concert were magical. I was aligned in my personal power. Everything seemed to go right. Then something put me in a bad mood and the magic dissipated, and it took a bit to rebound. That's life, though. Those who decide to stay on the ground crying over spilled milk are the ones who suffer. It gets easier to get up every time, much like muscle memory (or it's energy memory). But you have to take that first step to get off the floor, and singing while doing it doesn't hurt either.

An empath enjoys the experience of music, and the brain interprets it as a reward. It's a rewarding experience; a coping tool. Music helps dissolve the walls an empath may have built up. Music is an amazing healing gift for an empath, but because an empath absorbs the energy around them, be cautious. If you are an empath magnet like I am, remember to pull the big ol' bubble of white light around you at concerts. Carry crystals with you (kyanite, smoky quartz, or snowflake obsidian are great choices). And don't ever feel stuck! If you need to leave, leave.

CREATING A HEALTHIER RELATIONSHIP

Through my own failed relationships, I've learned some tips and tricks to make relationships healthier for an empath. Here's what I've learned so far:

- I need alone time. The people I love understand it's not about them, it's about me.

- I need sleep. Although I have no problem sleeping in the same bed as my husband, I sleep best when I can climb into bed solo and fall asleep by myself.

- I need to do activities on my own. This might include writing, reading, going for a walk, playing a game on my phone, etc.

- I need to be open and honest. When I'm feeling all the feelings, I have to be transparent or else I might end up supercharging a subject. This usually turns into an argument, and often, the issue was one that didn't need to be argued about in the first place.

- I need to be okay with making compromises. It's really not all about me.

- I need to play, laugh, watch comedies, and keep the energy positive. I can have serious conversations, of course, but it's important to balance them out with light and happy energy.

FEEL THE FEELINGS

Empaths often feel guilty for feeling all the feelings, but that's as silly as apologizing for having ten toes. Empaths feel like they are supposed to have all the answers, not the problems—they especially don't want to *be* a problem.

Chuck and I had saved for a couple of years to take a non-work trip with our friends. But only thirty hours into our vacation, I found myself sick in bed with what we believe was food poisoning. I began to travel down the rabbit hole of despair. I had spent all this money and here I was in my hotel room, sick. I felt awful in more ways than one. I felt awful for my friends, who felt awful for me. I felt awful for my husband, who worked so hard with me throughout the year. And I felt awful for myself because I really wanted some time to just play. I sent Chuck out of the room to have some fun, leaving me alone to be sick and try to sleep. I curled up in the fetal position and held my tummy. I didn't even have enough energy to cry. It wasn't long before Chuck returned to the hotel room.

"I can't have fun without you," he said, climbing into bed with me and snuggling the blanket up to my chin.

Again, I felt terrible about ruining everything. I began to cry.

"You know, you don't always have to be strong. Feel the feelings," he told me, hitting the clicker to turn the television on.

"Everyone's mad at me," I sniffled.

"Nobody is mad at you. Everyone just wants you better."

"I'm ruining everything." I continued my self-pity.

"You aren't," he said. "Everyone feels bad that you're sick. You've been pouring from an empty cup for so long. Now, I'm going to watch wrestling and you are going to rest. Tomorrow will be better."

The next day wasn't perfect, but it *was* better, and we were able to have a mostly okay vacation with fun memories—and some not-so-fun memories, but those came with lessons.

TOOLS FOR EMPATHS AND LOVE

There are many steps that an empath in love can take to be as healthy and happy as possible. I've included some suggestions for essential oils, crystals, and affirmations, as well as tips and a meditation.

MEDITATION EXERCISE FOR EMPATHS AND LOVE

Sit in a meditative position with the spine straight. Place your palms on your chest.

1. Inhale for three seconds, hold the breath for three seconds, and exhale for three seconds.

2. After doing this three times, say or sing, "Ra Ma Da Sa Sa Say So Hung."[7]

---

7. Ra is the sun, Ma is the moon, Da is the earth, Sa is infinity, Say is thou, and So Hung is "I am thou."

3. Visualize everyone that you feel needs your help, even those who may have hurt you or are hurting you. Imagine them sitting in front of you.

4. Visualize a light coming down from the sun and shining a beam of light over the people that need your help, charging them with strength, health, and harmony. At the same time, the light from the sun is charging you with an unlimited amount of strength, health, and harmony.

5. If you feel any energy from the people who need your help, push it back toward them so that their light can do the work in lieu of you doing their work.

6. Inhale for three seconds, hold for three seconds, and exhale for three seconds. Find contentment in the knowledge that you don't have to hold everyone's burdens.

PROTECTION TIPS FOR EMPATHS AND LOVE

Close your eyes and take a couple deep breaths in and out. Imagine a small child standing next to you. There is a giant bubble following the child. This bubble is dark and scary and filled with sadness, hurt, and fear. It holds awful memories. This bubble is constantly following the child and whispering (or maybe sometimes screaming) things like:

- I'm not good enough.
- I will never find love.
- I'm not worthy.

- I don't matter.

- Everyone hurts me.

Now, I want you to give that child a hug. Hold the child's hand. Together, pop that bubble and release all those negative stories.

Take another deep breath in. As you exhale, release any remaining heaviness. Embrace the child again and feel pure love.

Now, there is a new bubble following the child, but this bubble is filled with love, joy, laughter, and wishes that have come true.

See all the things you love floating within that bubble and feel peace all around you. The stories in this bubble say:

- I am good enough.

- I attract good people in my life.

- I am worthy of being loved.

- I matter.

- I am worthy.

See that child's bright smile? This right here is your doorway to inviting more positivity into your life. It is time for you to invite in happy memories filled with joy and love. You are now protected from lower-vibrational energy that creates false narratives.

ESSENTIAL OILS FOR EMPATHS AND LOVE

Never use essential oils directly on the skin. Always dilute essential oils with a carrier oil like almond oil, grapeseed oil, coconut oil, or olive oil. Essential oils are incredibly concentrated. A few drops are generally all that is needed. Practice aromatherapy by diffusing essential oils or sprinkling a few drops on a handkerchief or pillow.

- **Vanilla:** Vanilla is a relaxing and stress-relieving oil that soothes the body, mind, and spirit.

CRYSTALS FOR EMPATHS AND LOVE

Empaths are sensitive and very intuitive. Because of this, the empath absorbs both positive and negative energies from other people and their surroundings. Empaths naturally want to take care of people, and they often become drained in body, mind, and soul as a result. Crystals are an amazing tool to help. The best crystals for empaths protect the energy field (sometimes called an aura), shield an empath from negative emotions, and keep the empath grounded. You can wear these crystals as a piece of jewelry, put them in your purse or pocket, or lay them near you.

- **Rose Quartz:** This beautiful pink stone helps with true love, friendship, and harmonious relationships.
- **Rhodochrosite:** This stone is useful for discovering self-love, boosting self-confidence, and developing a higher self-esteem. The first step in finding love is learning to love yourself.

AFFIRMATIONS FOR EMPATHS AND LOVE

- The Universe guides me to healthy relationships.
- I am worthy of love.
- I attract caring and compassionate people.
- I make good choices about which people I allow in my life.

Conclusion

Every one of us is like a tree. We must nourish the trunk of the tree in order to have healthy limbs. Sometimes the limbs of the tree need to be cut off so there can be new growth. These limbs could be past loves, friendships that only lasted a season, a job opportunity that didn't work out, a current love that is unhealthy, issues with family, or financial problems. You see, empaths tend to nourish everyone else. They naturally help others, but they don't help themselves or allow others to help. Eventually, the empath realizes the trunk that used to be so strong has rotted. I hope this book helps you realize you can trim your limbs. Caring for your trunk—your very soul—strengthens every part of you, and then your limbs can grow stronger and bloom. It is only then that you can truly help others, after you have helped yourself.

As much as the crowded world might feel lonely, sometimes you simply need to adjust your focus and remove the backpacks you've been carrying for so long. You are sensitive to the visible and the invisible. Learning how to hold space for your own feelings is not only healthy, it's required. You may very well be a healer, but even healers need to take time to heal.

Dear empath, you are not wounded. You aren't cursed, you are gifted. You are an empath. You are valuable. You are someone. You are a warrior. You are beautiful. You are you.

Bibliography

Aron, Elaine N. *The Highly Sensitive Person: How to Thrive When the World Overwhelms You*. New York: Broadway Books, 1997.

Contreras, Cyndey. "Nicole Kidman Reveals the 'Disturbing' Side Effects She Endured from *The Undoing*." EOnline, January 11, 2021. https://www.eonline.com/news/1226077/nicole-kidman-reveals-the-disturbing-side-effects-she-endured-from-the-undoing.

Dyer, Judy. *Empaths and Narcissists: 2 Books in 1*. Pristine Publishing, 2020.

———. *The Highly Sensitive: How to Stop Emotional Overload, Relieve Anxiety, and Eliminate Negative Energy*. Self-published, CreateSpace, 2018. Kindle.

Evans, Hilary. *The SLI Effect: Street Lamp Interference*. Somerset, UK: ASSAP, 1993.

"Fierce Storm Slams Michigan Campground, Kills 1." *CBS News*, June 28, 2010. https://www.cbsnews.com/news/fierce-storm -slams-michigan-campground-kills-1/.

Hall, Judy. *The Crystal Bible: A Definitive Guide to Crystals*. Cincinnati, OH: Walking Stick Press, 2003.

Hinnant, Amanda. "10 Guilt-Free Strategies for Saying No." *Real Simple*, updated March 14, 2005. https://www.realsimple.com/ work-life/10-guilt-free-strategies-for-saying-no.

McCormick, Lorraine. *The Complete Aromatherapy Guidebook: A Comprehensive Reference of the Holistic Natural Healing Powers of Essential Oils for the Mind, Body, Spirit…and Comfort Zones*. Self-published, 2018.

Moon, Kimberly. *Psychic Empath: Secrets of Psychics and Empaths and a Guide to Developing Abilities Such as Intuition, Clairvoyance, Telepathy, Aura Reading, Healing Mediumship, and Connecting to Your Spirit Guides*. Self-published, 2019.

Nierenberg, Cari. "The Science of Intuition: How to Measure 'Hunches' and 'Gut Feelings.'" Live Science, May 20, 2016. https://www.livescience.com/54825-scientists-measure-intuition.html.

Orloff, Judith. *The Empath's Survival Guide: Life Strategies for Sensitive People*. Louisville, CO: Sounds True, 2018.

PsychReel. "Does Music Help Empaths? (A Complete Guide)." PsychReel, updated June 26, 2021. https://psychreel.com/ does-music-help-empaths/.

Thoreau, Henry David. Edited by Joseph Wood Krutch. *Walden and Other Writings*. New York: Bantam Books, 1962.

TO WRITE TO THE AUTHOR

If you wish to contact the author or would like more information about this book, please write to the author in care of Llewellyn Worldwide Ltd. and we will forward your request. Both the author and publisher appreciate hearing from you and learning of your enjoyment of this book and how it has helped you. Llewellyn Worldwide Ltd. cannot guarantee that every letter written to the author can be answered, but all will be forwarded. Please write to:

Kristy Robinett
℅ Llewellyn Worldwide
2143 Wooddale Drive
Woodbury, MN 55125-2989
Please enclose a self-addressed stamped envelope for reply,
or $1.00 to cover costs. If outside the U.S.A., enclose
an international postal reply coupon.

Many of Llewellyn's authors have websites with additional information and resources. For more information, please visit our website at http://www.llewellyn.com.